Case Studies
in Corrections

Sixth Edition

Case Studies
in Corrections

Sixth Edition

Bradley D. Edwards
Michael Braswell
Larry Miller
East Tennessee State University

WAVELAND
PRESS, INC.
Long Grove, Illinois

For information about this book, contact:
Waveland Press, Inc.
4180 IL Route 83, Suite 101
Long Grove, IL 60047-9580
(847) 634-0081
info@waveland.com
www.waveland.com

Previous editions of this book were published as *Human Relations and Corrections*.

10-digit ISBN 1-4786-3718-8
13-digit ISBN 978-1-4786-3718-9

Printed in the United States of America

7 6 5 4 3 2 1

Contents

CASE 1
Presentence Investigation: A Fair Shake?   10
A presentence investigator must write a report about a prominent citizen convicted of receiving stolen property. Will economic status affect the quality of justice?

CASE 2
The Court and Child Abuse   12
A family court judge must determine what is best for both the child and his parents who become abusive after drinking heavily.

CASE 3
Probation for Profit   14
A judge must decide whether to sentence two college women to a private or public probation agency.

CASE 4
Statutory Rapist   16
A district attorney is faced with the prosecution of a man for statutory rape. The law is clear, but the circumstances are clouded.

CASE 1
Bust or Parole?   68
An inmate coming up for parole witnesses another inmate beaten by a correctional officer who frames another inmate for the incident. Should she report the beating and the corruption in her cell block to the superintendent?

CASE 2
Six Months to Go   70
A young inmate learned about the Prison Rape Elimination Act in the law library. Four inmates brutally rape his cell mate and threaten that anyone who reports the crime will suffer the same fate.

CASE 3
An Expression of Grief   72
An inmate's father has died, and he cannot return home for the funeral because of his security classification despite being a model prisoner. While waiting to see the chaplain, he realizes he could escape. Will he?

CASE 4
Something for Nothing?   74
A young inmate in prison for the first time is being offered special favors by an older inmate.

CASE 5
What's for Supper?   76
An inmate leader must decide whether to endorse a protest that could lead to a disturbance concerning the poor quality of food served in the inmate dining hall.

CASE 6
Home Sweet Home   78
An older inmate who has been imprisoned three times for a total of 30 years is about to be released. Will he commit another crime?

Section IV
The Correctional Officer   85

Introduction   85
Employment   85
Correctional Officer and Inmate Attitudes   86
Prison Work   88
Summary   90

Preface

In film and television, corrections is often portrayed primarily as an environment in which wardens, correctional officers, and inmates interact—often violently. In reality, corrections is much more complex than that. Many other criminal justice professionals and civilians also interact with offenders. Judges sentence offenders, probation officers supervise them in the community, and correctional counselors and caseworkers provide treatment interventions. Educational specialists attempt to teach inmates basic education skills, while vocational instructors try to provide inmates with a marketable trade. Chaplains and clerics of all faiths conduct religious services and provide valuable pastoral counseling to inmate populations.

In community settings, offenders are sentenced to traditional probation as well as to alternative programs such as drug courts and house arrest. Innovations such as restorative justice are also available. These community corrections interventions may include victims of crime, the offender, criminal justice professionals, family, and other affected members of a community. When inmates have completed their sentences or are paroled, they typically return to communities from which they came and find that they need a number of support services to adjust to reentry. Increasingly, the justice system is turning to the volunteer services of former prisoners to assist in this process.

Case Studies in Corrections allows the reader to identify with various roles involved in the correctional process. The roles of inmate, judge, probation officer, correctional officer, counselor, and administrator are representative of critical relationships that enhance or distract from the correctional system's rehabilitative potential. The authors contend that effective relationships are the major contributors to correctional success.

The cases in this book allow the reader to analyze real life situations that are part of the correctional process. As with all life situations, the solutions to the case studies presented are not black and white. It is important to understand that corrections is only one part of the criminal justice system. Law enforcement, the court system, and corrections are interrelated and must work together toward the goal of reducing crime. What might seem like a common-sense solution to an issue that corrections agencies face might have unexpected consequences for law enforcement, the court system, or our communities.

A number of new cases have been added to this edition, including contemporary topics such as police brutality, domestic violence, mental health, immigration, and cyberbullying. All names and scenarios portrayed in this book are fictitious. Any similarities the cases may have to any real persons or situations are strictly coincidental.

Acknowledgements

We want to thank the students and colleagues in academic and agency settings who have provided valuable input regarding suggestions for case topics and other ways of improving this book. We would like to give special thanks to Hannah Medford for her efforts. Finally, we would like to thank our editor, Carol Rowe, for her useful suggestions.

SECTION I

The Court and Corrections

The courts have a greater impact on corrections than perhaps any other component of the criminal justice system. Whether dealing with the civil rights of prison inmates or abused children, courts interpret the laws that are the foundation of our system of justice. After a brief introduction to some of the responsibilities of the courts, this section includes eight cases from the viewpoint of various court professionals. For example, as a family court judge you will have to use your judicial discretion concerning a child-abuse case. In another case, you will need to decide as a presentence investigator the appropriate purpose and limits of a presentence investigation report and its consequences for a group of juveniles who contributed to the suicide of a friend. The other six cases cover additional situations encountered by court employees.

Introduction

The criminal and appellate courts are, in a sense, the hub of the criminal justice system around which all the other components revolve. The remainder of the criminal justice system is subject to decisions made in the courts. Police procedures are governed by court decisions regarding arrests, search and seizure, and interpretation of existing statutes. The correctional system also is affected by court case law decisions about the civil rights of prisoners, right to treatment, methods of treatment, and institutional procedures (Palmer, 2015).

Criminal court cases are often viewed as melodramatic episodes or contests between two opposing forces vying to prove the technical guilt or innocence of a defendant (Kappeler & Potter, 2018). Prosecutors usually depict the evil that the defendant allegedly committed. Prosecutors may attempt to encourage the jury to see the defendant as a destructive

1

individual needing punishment. Defense attorneys frequently make a play for the jury's sympathy by portraying the defendant as a victim of society, raised in an abusive family environment, or the target of harassment by law enforcement officials. In some cases, the defense may also attempt to make the jury angry that the defendant was set up by his or her accusers. The judge is a referee making decisions on motions and testimony. Judges try to weigh all the consequences of a decision. If a judge makes a wrong decision, there is an appeals process to assess the legality of the decision.

Juries consist of individuals who usually know little about the criminal justice system (Somin, 2014). Their viewpoints are shaped by media depictions of high-profile criminal cases and popular television crime dramas (Surette, 2015). For example, the prevalence of DNA and other forensic evidence in popular crime dramas have influenced jurors who expect a higher level of physical evidence than is typically involved in criminal cases (Hawkins & Scherr, 2017). Attorneys for both the prosecution and the defense will try to use the juror's lack of knowledge to their advantage in choosing a jury and presenting their case. These attorneys will often attempt to select a jury who they feel will be most sympathetic to their arguments (Lieberman, 2011).

A basic concept of the criminal justice system in the United States tips the scales of justice in favor of the freedom of an offender rather than risk the conviction of an innocent person. The only requirement in finding an accused individual not guilty is a reasonable doubt. The government must abide by several due process protections to ensure a fair trial. Failure to do so not only could result in a wrongful conviction but could also be challenged at the appellate court level in an attempt to rectify the error. It is ultimately the responsibility of both the prosecution and defense to ensure that a fair trial takes place and that only the guilty are convicted.

Our laws have always allowed for the incarceration of serious violent offenders and discretionary options of incarceration and probation for other felonies. Over the last quarter of the twentieth century, concern increased over the frequency of violent crime. Legislators, in order to appease their constituencies, supported mandatory sentencing and incarceration for a number of serious offenses. In most states the penalties for criminal violence increased, while provisions for parole and other alternate sentencing decreased. While it is debatable whether these laws accomplished desired goals, they definitely resulted in overcrowded correctional institutions (Carson, 2018). In response to this reality, judges and correctional personnel have focused more heavily on nonviolent offenders for sentencing alternatives. As the public's view toward "get tough" policies have declined in recent years (Ramirez, 2013), several innovative programs have been developed to constrain the growth of the prison population.

Presentence Diversion

Under mandatory or determinate sentencing, judges had little discretion. If the defendant was found guilty, the law prescribed the length of the prison sentence. Changes in sentencing laws have restored some judicial discretion. Judges have a broad range of choices, particularly when the offender is nonviolent. Some of the alternatives to incarceration are electronic house arrest, pretrial diversion, drug courts, day reporting, and restitution.

In deciding a sentence, the duration of a sentence, or whether to place an offender on probation, a judge may utilize a presentence investigation report. A presentence investigation is generally prepared by a probation officer, court officer, or social worker. The report might include information regarding the current and previous offenses by the offender, the offender's attitude toward the offense, family history, educational history, occupational history, habits (e.g., alcohol and drug usage, gambling, etc.), and the offender's physical and mental health. A risk assessment score is also often provided which that gives the judge an indication of whether the offender is more or less likely than the average offender to reoffend. The report usually concludes with summaries and recommendations (Freiburger & Hilinski, 2011).

Risk-assessment tools were designed to provide an actuarial evaluation of the risk to public safety when deciding on probation or early release. Some researchers believe the static factors incorporated in modern risk models such as demographics, substance-abuse history, criminality of associates and friends, and criminality of one's parents violate constitutional protections (Cui, 2016). Risk scores include a number of factors that are not related to the crime committed (Starr, 2014). In essence, the factors profile the offender.

Downsizing the system through relief from mandatory sentences was well intentioned, but racial and economic disparities remain. Risk assessment weights criminal history heavily (including arrests that did not result in convictions), and many alternatives to detention specify that defendants with extensive criminal histories are not eligible (Kappeler & Potter, 2018). Allowing judges more discretion can also work against the disadvantaged. Judges who look at a defendant's education and employment as guidelines for granting leniency may unknowingly act on their biases. If an alternative to incarceration depends on the participation of family members, a judge who views a household as dysfunctional may decide detention is more appropriate. The first beneficiaries of downsizing the system are those who have somewhere else to go.

Probation is among the most widely used sentencing alternatives. Probation often includes a suspended sentence, granting conditional freedom to an offender who meets prescribed requirements (Latessa & Smith, 2015). The probationer must be supervised by a probation officer, follow strict rules, and in some cases attend counseling sessions with probation or other treatment professionals. Community service and restitution may also be a part of the considerations of probation. Judges may impose a wide array of probation conditions with which an offender must comply or face the likelihood of incarceration. For the community, probation is much more economical than incarceration. The public sometimes regards probation as too permissive, slapping offenders on the wrist while ignoring crime victims (Stohr & Walsh, 2019). However, the major purpose of probation is not to punish but to treat and provide guidance for the offender. Offenders placed on probation should be those who are of low risk to the community and have the potential to become law-abiding citizens. Probation is not an appropriate option for the violent criminal whose incarceration is primarily for the protection of the community.

The level of supervision provided by the probation officer largely depends on the offender's risk of reoffending. Some low-risk probationers are only required to call into the probation department periodically or to use a kiosk to provide the type of information traditionally given to a probation officer (Ahlin, Hagen, Harmon, & Crosse, 2016). Medium-risk offenders are often required to meet with a probation officer approximately once per month and may be subject to home visits and drug tests. The highest risk offenders are often sentenced to intensive probation, which involves a much closer level of supervision.

Offenders who violate probation could be subject to the revocation of the probation sentence and face the possibility of imprisonment. Recently, many states have begun to experiment with graduated sanctions for probation violations. Graduated sanctions may include increasing the required amount of community service hours, electronic monitoring or more intensive treatment options, and research has found these sanctions to be as effective as jail time (Wodahl, Boman, & Garland, 2015). Further, offenders appear to view the graduated sanctions as similarly punitive compared to jail time (Wodahl, Ogle, Kadleck, & Gerow, 2013).

Juvenile Courts

The juvenile court is a special statutory court enacted by local and/or state legislation. Only a few states currently have a statewide juvenile justice system. Juvenile courts are usually controlled by a municipality and/or county government. The philosophy of the juvenile court is to care for, protect, and reform juveniles. Traditionally, the juvenile court has not been viewed as a court of punishment, although over time it appears to have become more like the adult system.

The terminology used in juvenile court varies from that of adult court. For instance, juvenile offenders do not commit crimes, they commit *delinquent acts*. Juveniles are *taken into custody* rather than arrested. A *petition* is the equivalent of an indictment. A trial is called an *adjudicatory hearing*, which is often followed by a *dispositional hearing*, the equivalent of a sentencing hearing in the adult system. A sentence is a *commitment*, and *detention* is the equivalent of incarceration (Shelden & Troshynski, 2019). Finally, the records of juveniles are often sealed or expunged so that they cannot be accessed after the child becomes an adult (Shah, Fine, & Gullen, 2014).

In 1899, the first juvenile court was established in Cook County, Illinois, based on the concept of *parens patriae* that grants the state the power to serve as guardian. The idea of the juvenile court removing young offenders from adult court and emphasizing an informal, non-adversarial approach spread quickly throughout the United States. Cases were treated as civil rather than criminal. Because of the non-criminal approach to juvenile offenders, many of the due process rights of adult offenders were omitted from juvenile court procedures (Wills, 2017). The informality of the juvenile court prevailed for over 60 years. Since the *Gault* decision in 1967, juvenile courts have generally applied due process rights to juvenile offenders (Landess, 2016). Table 1 illustrates the major due process court decisions.

In 45 states, the maximum age of juvenile court jurisdiction is 17. In five states (GA, MI, MO, TX, and WI), the maximum age is 16 (Teigen, 2017). All states have transfer laws that allow or require offenders to be prosecuted as adults for specific serious offenses. There are four forms of transfer laws to adult court. Under statutory exclusion, state law specifies certain classes of cases over which only adult criminal court has jurisdiction; murder and serious violent felony cases are most commonly excluded from juvenile court. Under judicially controlled transfer, all cases begin in juvenile court but can be waived by that court to adult court. Under prosecutorial discretion transfer, the prosecutor decides whether to file charges in juvenile or adult court. Some states have both statutory exclusion and prosecutorial discretion. About half the states have "once an adult, always an adult" laws. Any juvenile previously prosecuted in adult court will be prosecuted for any new offense (serious or not) as an adult. Many critics have argued that processing juveniles in adult court could have detrimental effects for the child. There are fewer rehabilitative programs in adult facilities, and youth incarcerated with adults are at greater risk for rape, assault, and suicide (Merlo & Benekos, 2017).

The juvenile court has jurisdiction over many other juvenile matters. Status offenses involve behavior that would not be prosecuted if

Table 1   Major Court Decisions Affecting Due Process Rights for Juveniles

Date	Court Case Citation	Court Decision
1966	*Kent v. United States* 383 US 541	Before a judge transfers a case from juvenile court to adult court, a juvenile is entitled to a hearing and has the right to counsel. If transferred, there must be a written statement giving the reasons for the waiver, and defense counsel must have access to all records and reports used in reaching the waiver decision.
1967	*In re Gault* 387 US 1	At an adjudicatory hearing, juvenile court procedures must include written notice of the charges, the right to counsel, privilege against self-incrimination, the right to cross-examine accusers, a transcript of the proceedings, and the right to appellate review.
1970	*In re Winship* 397 US 358	The due process clause of the Fourteenth Amendment requires that determination of delinquency must meet the same standard of "beyond a reasonable doubt" required in the adult system, replacing the lesser standard of "a preponderance of the evidence."
1971	*McKeiver v. Pennsylvania* 403 US 528	Trial by jury was traditionally denied to juveniles. The ruling stated jury trials for juveniles were admissible but not mandatory. Ten states currently grant the right to a jury trial if requested; six states grant the right under certain conditions.
1975	*Breed v. Jones* 421 US 519	Juveniles are protected against double jeopardy by the Fifth Amendment. A child cannot be adjudicated in juvenile court then transferred to an adult court to be tried on the same offense.
1979	*Smith v. Daily Mail Publishing* 443 US 97	As long as information is legally obtained, a state cannot restrict a newspaper from publishing a juvenile offender's name unless the restriction serves a substantial state interest.
2005	*Roper v. Simmons* 543 US 551	It is unconstitutional for juveniles who commit capital offenses while under the age of 18 to receive a death penalty sentence.
2010	*Graham v. Florida* 560 US 48	It is a violation of the Eight Amendment for juveniles to be sentenced to life without parole for a non-homicidal offense.
2012	*Miller v. Alabama* 567 US __	It is unconstitutional to sentence juvenile (under the age of 18 at the time of the crime) homicide offenders to mandatory life without parole.
2016	*Montgomery v. Louisiana* 577 US __	The decision in *Miller v. Alabama* established a substantive constitutional rule that applies retroactively. The Constitution treats children differently from adults for the purposes of sentencing.

committed by an adult; the behavior is prohibited only because of the age (status) of the offender (e.g., possession of alcohol or tobacco, playing gaming machines, curfew violations, running away, truancy, etc.). The juvenile court, or in some cases the family court, may also have presiding jurisdiction over child-abuse cases, divorce settlements involving children, and other civil matters involving children. The juvenile court may have some jurisdiction over adults whose acts, encouragement, indifference, or indulgence are the cause of a child's problem. Research has shown that exposure to abuse and other maltreatment increases the child's risk of engaging in delinquency and future criminal behavior (Barrett, Ju, Katsiyannis, & Zhang, 2015; Topitzes, Mersky, & Reynolds, 2012). For this reason, jurisdiction over adults who contribute to the delinquency or dependency of children has been vested in the juvenile courts of many states. Other situations involving both children and adults include guardianship, child labor law violations, nonsupport and desertion, paternity suits, and adoptions. In some jurisdictions, these courts may also be called family courts rather than juvenile courts.

Diversionary Practices

The meaning of *diversion* is often confusing, perhaps because there are so many different types of diversion programs available. For example, diversion can be initiated by the police prior to an arrest, by the prosecution after booking, or by court officials through the use of a problem-solving court (Center for Health and Justice, 2013). Many diversion programs are designed for offenders who are mentally ill, have committed low-level crimes, or have committed specific crimes, such as domestic violence or drug offenses. Each type of diversion involves some type of treatment, drug testing, or counseling, with the goal of rehabilitating the offender and dismissing the charges after successful completion of the program (Camilletti, 2010).

Despite the courts' growing use of diversionary programs, such a trend is not without opposition, especially in the juvenile arena. Nearly 45% of juvenile cases are dealt with informally (Hockenberry & Puzzanchera, 2017). Of these, many situations are simply resolved with a warning or brief counseling. However, it is also common to address the underlying needs of the child through some form of individual or family-based treatment, restorative justice, or teen court (Schwalbe, Gearing, MacKenzie, Brewer, & Ibrahim, 2012; Smokowski et al., 2017). Critics view these practices as potentially harmful. They caution that while such programs may be well intended, their ultimate effect is *net widening*, pulling juveniles into the criminal justice system. They maintain that diversion programs often target behavior that would otherwise not be considered criminal or processed by the juvenile justice system at all (Bechard, Ireland, Berg, & Vogel, 2011). Therefore, the court system may actually be intervening in more situations than would be the case if the programs did not exist. Finally, some scholars worry that a charismatic policy maker or judge could promote the use of a particular diversion program or a courtroom culture could decide that certain youths should be diverted and others not (Mears, 2017).

Similar concerns surface regarding adult diversionary programs, such as drug courts. Critics find the lack of uniformity (criteria for admission, type of treatment programming available, and impact on sentencing) troubling (Shelden, Brown, Miller, & Fritzler, 2016). They also question whether the courts, while diverting some people from incarceration, might actually be widening the net of social control by supervising people who might not have been processed by the courts.

The large number of court cases and offenders in correctional institutions, and the fact that many offenders could be eligible for diversion, support the increased use of alternatives to incarceration. Almost half of all arrestees could be sanctioned more effectively without being sentenced to jail or prison. Keep in mind that there are far more petty crimes committed in the United States compared to serious felonies and that many are committed by people with mental health issues or substance abuse problems. Although few serious violent crimes in which weapons are used may be diverted, many misdemeanor offenses may be handled appropriately outside the criminal justice system.

As prison overcrowding continues to strain government budgets, legislators and correctional administrators have sought innovative correctional methods to reduce inmate populations. Various reform efforts have included intermediate sanctions such as house arrest and electronic monitoring (Yeh, 2010). One of the fastest growing reform efforts is justice reinvestment. This model allows states to identify ways to reduce their prison populations and reinvest the cost savings into evidence-based programs such as improved community corrections, substance abuse treatment, and victim's services (LaVigne et al., 2014). These reforms seem to be working, as the prison population growth has declined from peak levels (Carson, 2018).

Summary

The courts have a tremendous impact on the criminal justice system as a whole and the correctional component in particular. Procedures for law enforcement and methods for corrections have largely come as a result of statutes, cases, and constitutional law interpretations of higher courts. Judges and other court officials use their discretion to determine the best outcome for each case. Because of a broad range of judicial alternatives to sentencing of criminal offenders, many judges rely on presentence investigation reports and risk assessment tools. Such reports assist judges in determining sentence, probation, or treatment. Many courts are resorting to formalized diversionary practices for convicted offenders. Probation has become the most popular form of diversion. Other forms of diversionary programs have shown success in offender treatment and decreasing recidivism rates.

Juvenile courts have multiple roles and responsibilities. In addition to adjudicating juvenile offenders, the juvenile court may have jurisdiction in cases where adults contribute to the delinquency of minors, family conflicts, civil cases involving children, and child abuse. As illustrated in the cases to follow, there are often no easy answers available to resolve these cases. Court officials must use the tools available to them and their best judgement to determine the most appropriate action.

The increased use of diversionary programs in the court system creates new responsibilities for correctional workers, including the need for increased counseling. These programs incorporate the community in helping offenders. While there have been promising results from some of the alternative practices, critics argue that the courts may be extending the reach of the criminal justice system rather than diminishing its control. Evidence-based evaluations are needed to insure that justice reinvestments are improving the correctional process.

Case 1

Presentence Investigation
A Fair Shake?

The community was shocked when the arrest was made by the state bureau of criminal investigation. The sheriff had not even been aware that an investigation was under way, much less that such a prominent citizen as Johnny James was involved.

The outcome of the trial has never seemed to be in doubt. The public was outraged that a former state's attorney was involved in receiving stolen property and disposing of it in conspiracy with a convicted felon. The stolen items, worth tens of thousands of dollars each, included heavy equipment that had been stolen from construction sites, stashed out on the attorney's ranch, and ultimately disposed of through a third party. It was a lucrative racket and probably would have gone undetected had not one of the buyers offered to sell a bulldozer back to the same contractor from whom it had been stolen. The rightful owner quickly identified the bulldozer by the unusual mechanical modification that had been made before the equipment was stolen from a roadside work site. The resultant investigation revealed altered serial numbers and the criminal enterprise.

You know writing the presentence investigation is going to be tough. There are those who may soften their criticisms because of current associations with Johnny James; others will want to "hang" him because they believe a public official, even an ex-public official, ought to set a moral example in the community and certainly not be a "fence" for stolen goods.

The investigation progresses quickly, and Johnny James is now out on bail. James had been a fine high school athlete, president of his class, and had attended the best law school in the state. He soon established himself as a smart lawyer and an ambitious and successful businessperson. Fifteen years later, he owned a controlling interest in a farm implement company, a thriving automobile business, and an interest in a large motel. He is considered a friend of law enforcement, hosting a large annual party for area law officers. He is also a model member of the community in most respects, with strong church affiliations and membership in several respected and prestigious civic organizations. His wife heads a local hospital volunteer effort, and there is no indication of any rift within the family. Aside from strong contrasting opinions of local citizens, there is no indication of danger to citizens if this particular offender continues to reside in the community.

However, one matter bothers you about this investigation. Why should this "big time" lawyer who was involved in the theft of thousands of dollars worth of private property be out on bail? He may never even serve one day of "hard time," while an ordinary thief would no doubt receive a more traditional sentence in the state penitentiary. You feel that crime is crime, whether white collar or not.

You wonder if you should look deeper into Johnny James' background for indications of a pattern that might predict continued criminal behavior. Perhaps his campaign contributions and his political connections should also be investigated. You know for a fact that his motel is frequented by out-of-town prostitutes who are never arrested. This kind of information could influence the judge and might even result in a prison sentence.

Questions for Discussion

Regarding the case of Johnny James, you are painfully and somewhat angrily aware of the different qualities of justice available to offenders according to their economic status. The question lingers: "Why should James have a better chance for judicial consideration than a more common thief?" On the other hand, although his crime was quite serious, up until this offense Johnny James had apparently led a productive life well within legal boundaries. Should you, as the presentence investigator, dig deeper into James' past or limit your queries to the specific case with which he is involved? What are the rehabilitation prospects for this particular offender?

Case 2

The Court and Child Abuse

As a lawyer you always enjoyed private practice. However, after 10 years of successful practice, you decided to enter public service and politics. You and your family realized that public service does not have the financial rewards of a private practice, but your 10-year law practice solidified your financial situation. Over the years you have made some important personal connections and a good name for yourself. On your first attempt at public service, you were elected county prosecutor. Being a prosecutor meant practicing law differently; your new job was to convict people in the name of the state rather than defending them from prosecution. Of the variety of cases you prosecuted, some naturally stirred your interests more than others. Because you are a family man, the crime of child abuse was one of the crimes that made you press harder. You always prosecuted abusive parents to the full extent of the law and had their children removed to a nonthreatening environment. Trials for this offense always proved to be an emotional experience for you.

Your career as county prosecutor progressed rapidly. Eventually you were appointed a family court judge, a position which again proved to be a different world. You now have to evaluate facts objectively, rather than approach the case primarily from a prosecutor's or defense lawyer's point of view. Your first case of child abuse as judge proves to be a very difficult experience. The family is very prominent in the community. Both husband and wife are successful professionals, highly regarded by their colleagues. The police discovered the abuse as a result of a family disturbance call. The abuse had apparently been taking place for a short time, and because of the family's community standing it had been covered up. The abuse seemed to have resulted from marital problems that had led both parents to heavy drinking. During an argument between the couple, their 7-year-old son interrupted them. From then on, they focused and projected their problems onto the child.

The actual physical abuse was usually a belt strap across the back of the young boy. The psychological damage to the youth as a result of his parents' behavior was, of course, impossible to measure. You are also troubled by another subtle aspect of this particular case. Apparently the child spends most of the time when he is not in school with a variety of sitters, typically seeing his parents for one or two hours each night. He also frequently spends his weekends with grandparents.

You are not the county prosecutor or defense attorney now. You are the judge, and you must try to do what is best for all concerned, especially the boy. Should you take him out of his home? If you do, you will be taking him away from the place he lives and from his natural parents. His parents are in a financial position to do a great deal for their son, whereas a government agency could not. More important, the boy does love his parents and seems to want to stay with them. On the other hand, if you do not remove him from the home, he could be subjected to even more severe abuse. Another option would be to grant custody to the grandparents, but you wonder whether this would actually stop the abuse or simply generate more strain within the family. The court experience might open the eyes of the parents to their need for professional help in solving their problems and child-abuse tendencies, but there is no way to be sure. Do you take the child out of his home, or do you let the parents keep custody and hope that the child will not be subjected to further abuse?

Questions for Discussion

In this particular case, you must think of the parents as well as the abused child. Could a diversion program including family counseling and psychotherapy rehabilitate the parents? If you decide on this course of action, what specific recommendations should you make regarding the family's treatment program? Have the parents stopped abusing alcohol? What course of action would best help the parents rethink their priorities?

Case 3

Probation for Profit

You pore over the presentence evaluation for two intoxicated college girls, one a DUI and the other who tried to elude police officers. Neither girl has any prior arrests; both are nursing majors at the local college. As the judge, you must decide whether to sentence them to the state probation agency or to place them in a private probation agency (Second Chance, Inc.). Through social media and advertising, the private agency touts its progressive approach and impressive array of programs: alcohol and drug intervention, moral values instruction, individual and group therapy, and follow-up services every six months. You must admit that on paper they do look impressive. The state agency's services are more traditional and limited. In addition, the attorney representing the two students indicated that they would prefer to be referred to the private agency.

You have been a judge for 10 years, and you take your job seriously. You believe in both consequences for breaking the law and also in doing the least harm to young adults regarding their future prospects. It would be easy enough to accede to the young women's wishes, yet you find yourself becoming increasingly uneasy about what you are hearing through the grapevine about Second Chance, Inc. At best, the private agency seems to highly exaggerate the services it offers. At worst, they could be little more than a for-profit collection agency, a cash cow for the executive director who owns the agency and his program director. They both make six figure incomes, while they pay their case managers meager wages. Especially troubling is their "intensive 24/7" program option where offenders who can afford higher fees can cut their probation time by 50%. Their primarily middle-class clients seem pleased with their services, yet your instinct warns you that there are problems below the surface.

The State's diversion program includes monthly contacts, group meetings, and community service on the weekends. The two girls' families prefer the private agency and can afford the fees, but is that the best option in the interest of justice and rehabilitation?

Questions for Discussion

As the judge, are there any other options? Should you allow your personal beliefs about the private agency to influence the sentence you impose on the two coeds? How should private community corrections agencies be controlled and/or monitored to insure that they are providing the services that they claim to offer? What are the ethical criteria for sentencing decisions such as the one the judge is preparing to make? Can justice be "bought" in our criminal justice system? Do judges, other criminal justice professionals, and the system itself have a moral obligation to ensure that private corrections agencies provide meaningful and effective correctional services? What are some ways in which such agencies could be monitored and evaluated in order to make them more accountable?

Case 4

Statutory Rapist

You are an assistant district attorney in a small circuit-court region. The region consists of three counties with an average population of 80,000 per county. The community you serve is primarily composed of middle-class people with middle-class values. Having come from a large city, you are particularly impressed with the small-town atmosphere and relaxed way of life.

The district attorney general hired you straight out of law school two years ago. You felt that a job with the D.A.'s office would be an excellent opportunity to gain needed experience and develop a reputation as a good lawyer. Your ambition is to enter the political arena and perhaps run for state representative in a couple of years. You have stressed a "law and order" image in order to accomplish your career ambitions.

As you prepare to look over the court docket for tomorrow's cases, your secretary advises you that Sheriff's Investigator Jim Wainwright is waiting to see you.

"Jim, come in. I was going to call you about our burglary case tomorrow. You didn't have to come over here in person today."

"Thanks, Bill, but I need to talk with you about another matter. You know, we arrested a young man by the name of Fred Granger a couple of days ago for rape and I wanted to fill you in on some details."

Fred Granger is a 22-year-old white male who works in a nearby factory. He has a high school education and no prior felony arrests or convictions, but he does have a previous conviction for DUI two years ago and one for possession of marijuana three years ago. He has been charged with the rape of a 16-year-old girl under state code 37–1–2702:

> Any adult who carnally knows a child under the age of seventeen by sexual intercourse shall be guilty of the offense of statutory rape. The punishment for same shall be not less than five years nor more than ten years in the state penitentiary without the possibility of

16

parole. It shall be no defense that the child consented to the act or that the defendant was ignorant of the age of the child.

The punishment for this offense is no different than for the crime of forcible rape in your state. Fred Granger was arrested on a complaint from the parents of the 16-year-old girl named Debbie. Fred had picked Debbie up for a date, went to the lake, and had sexual intercourse with her. It was a clear violation of the law and an apparently easy conviction, since Fred admitted to arresting officers that he had sex with Debbie.

"So, what information do you have for me, Jim?" you ask.

"We've obtained statements from everyone involved. This is basically what went down. Fred knew Debbie's sister, Nina, who is 20 years old. Fred and Nina had gone out before on a couple of dates in the past and have had intercourse. It seems Nina and her younger sister, Debbie, have the reputation of being 'easy.' Anyway, Fred called Nina for a date and Nina wasn't at home. Debbie answered the phone and started flirting with Fred. Fred asked Debbie if she wanted to go with him to the lake and Debbie agreed. Debbie apparently wore a very revealing bathing suit and 'came on' to Fred. They had intercourse and Fred dropped Debbie back home. Debbie's parents inquired about her activities for the day and Debbie told them everything, even about the sex. That's when we got the call. Fred states that he thought Debbie was over 17 and that Debbie consented to having sex with him. Debbie supports this story. Both of them were drinking beer at the lake."

"Yes, well, I see. But, it's no defense for Fred to be ignorant of her actual age and no defense for him that Debbie consented. He probably got her drunk anyway. The law is clear on this matter," you advise.

"Yes, I know, Bill. But this Debbie has a reputation of being very promiscuous. She is very open about the fact that she consented. She now says she's in love with Fred. Needless to say, her parents aren't very happy about her attitude, but they seem to have very little control over her or her sister. Besides, anyone who's seen Debbie could make a mistake about her age."

The investigator pulls out and shows you a recent photograph of Debbie. The photograph surprises you. You had never seen the victim, but in the photograph Debbie looks well over 20 years old.

"Hey, she does look at least 20," you respond. "She certainly would have fooled me."

"Yeah. Anyone might assume that," the investigator replies.

Looking over the statements that the investigator brought, you begin to feel uneasy about the case. In a legal sense, Fred is a criminal. He violated the state law. He has no legal defense. The girl is under 17, which means she cannot testify that she consented. The fact that she has had intercourse before also cannot be used as a defense for Fred. It seems to be an open-and-shut case. Fred is looking at 5 to 10 years with no chance of parole. Even if he got the minimum five years, it is still a stiff punishment for ignorance. You decide to call on the district attorney general for advice.

"Yes, Bill. I see why you are concerned. It seems to me you have three options here. One, you could *nolle prosequi* (no longer prosecute) the case. Two, you could reduce charges through a plea bargain arrangement. Or, three, you could prosecute to the fullest extent of the law. It's basically a choice between legal ethics and personal ethics. Legal ethics would dictate that you prosecute to the fullest. A crime by statutes has been committed and you are sworn to uphold the law. In that sense, it would not be legally ethical for you to *nolle prosequi* or plea bargain when you have such a strong case. And, if you did, it might affect your political career. On the other hand, your personal ethics dictate that this Fred fellow is not a typical criminal. He's guilty of stupidity, maybe. But, apparently when you look at Debbie, you can see why. If you prosecuted the case, the jury might see Debbie the way Fred saw her and acquit him. But that is a big chance to take. Juries are unpredictable and you can't bring up the fact that she 'looks' of age. I don't know, Bill. It's your decision. I'll back you on whatever you decide."

Questions for Discussion

How would the community and justice be served by prosecuting this case? How could the correctional system "rehabilitate" Fred; or for that matter, help Debbie? Do you think the jury would nullify the law by acquitting Fred? What legal defenses does Fred have? What would be the consequences of *nolle prosequi* or plea bargaining? With the increasing use of sex-offender registries, it is probable that Fred would have to register as a sex offender even if a plea deal was reached. What would be the collateral consequences for Fred if he was found guilty?

Case 5

What's Best for the Family? What's Best for the Wife?

You are a court caseworker en route to a home visit on a spousal assault probation case. Six weeks ago Terrance O'Dell was arrested for wife battering. Barbara O'Dell called police to "stop her husband from hurting her." In your state, the victim of spousal abuse does not have to press charges. The police can make an arrest if they have sufficient probable cause to believe an assault took place. Barbara did not testify at court, but the responding officer testified about Barbara's swollen face and bloody nose. The result was a mandatory thirty days jail time and one year probation.

Terrance has just been released from the county jail and is back home with his wife and two small children. You are required to make periodic home visits to determine if the rules of probation are being followed and the victim is not endangered again. As you pull up to the O'Dell residence in a low-income neighborhood, you note that the house and yard are neat and well kept.

Barbara comes to the door.

"Hello, Ms. Roberts. Please come in and have a seat."

"Is Mr. O'Dell here?" you ask, looking around the small living room area.

"Here I am. I was out back changin' oil in the car. Sorry I might be a little dirty."

"That's alright. As I said on the phone, I just wanted to stop by to check to see if everything was going smoothly since your release." You fumble through your attaché case, looking for the case file.

"Everything's just fine now, isn't it honey?" Terrance hugs his wife around the shoulders.

"Oh yes. All is well now, thank you," Barbara replies a little nervously.

"Let's see now, Mr. O'Dell. The court has ordered that you undergo alcohol counseling at the Alcohol and Drug Treatment Center. When is your next appointment there?"

"Why, I was there yesterday to check in after my release. Had to fill out some papers and stuff. I'm supposed to see my counselor next Thursday.".

You ask, "So, how is the alcohol problem?"

"Haven't had a drop in over a month now. It was rough while I was in jail but I don't need it anymore, isn't that right honey?" Terrance looks over toward his wife.

Barbara smiles and nervously nods her head in the affirmative.

"Mr. O'Dell, would you mind if I talked with your wife in private, please?"

"No, no, not at all. I've got to finish up on the car outside. But she'll tell you everything's just fine now," Terrance pats Barbara on the shoulder as he leaves.

"Now, Ms. O'Dell. How are things . . . really?"

Barbara responds nervously, "Just like he said. Everything's fine now."

"Doesn't sound like you are too sure."

"Well, to be honest with you, he did get a little drunk yesterday after he got out, but he was under a lot of stress. He lost his job at the truck company because he was in jail so long. But he might be able to get on at this construction company next week."

"Did he assault you or threaten to hurt you in any manner when he got drunk?" you inquire.

"Well . . . no, not really. He fussed a lot. But he's got a right to, you know. It was my fault that he got in jail and lost his job. I should have never called the police. But, at the time, I was afraid for the kids, you know?"

"Yes, I think I do. You know that if he threatens you or the children we can have him locked up again. You don't have to put up with this," you advise.

"No, no. I wouldn't want that. We can't afford him to go back to jail. Like he said last night, if he went back, me and the kids would have nothin', no money, no food, nothin'. We couldn't live without him to support us."

As you leave the O'Dell's house you cannot help but feel uneasy about the situation. It appears to you that the time Mr. O'Dell spent in jail was not particularly helpful for his problem or his family. As you walk to your car, you notice a neighbor washing his car next door.

"Excuse me, sir. I'm Officer Jane Roberts with court services. I wonder if I could ask you about your neighbors, the O'Dells?" You show your credentials.

"Are you going to put that asshole back in jail? I came close to calling the cops last night after I seen him curse poor Mrs. O'Dell on the front porch. That guy's dangerous. If I was her I'd shoot him, especially when he starts on the kids," the neighbor states angrily.

You realize now that the problem is still present in the O'Dell household. You have the power to revoke Mr. O'Dell's probation with probable cause. However, maybe it would be best to wait to see if the alcohol counseling and probation will do any good. Still, if you wait until it is too late. . . .

Questions for Discussion

How long should you wait to see if things really do get better in the O'Dell household? Do you think revoking probation would do any good? What if you waited and Ms. O'Dell or the children were seriously hurt—would you be liable? What are the advantages and disadvantages of mandatory arrest and jail time for spousal assault cases?

Case 6

Lost Boys, Inc.

It says it right there on your letterhead—"Judge Sharon W. Elliott, Juvenile Court, Fourth District." For the last seven years, you have done what you could to give the troubled youth of your district all the help you could find within the limits of the law. The single mother of a teenage daughter and grown son, you know how hard it is to keep boys and girls positively motivated and out of trouble. You want to judge wisely, humanely, and fairly. Sometimes, as in the case before you, there is no clear answer.

Joey Martinez is a 15-year-old boy appearing before you for the second time. He's more of a nuisance than a danger to the community. Like many a young man with a bit of a chip on his shoulder, Joey wants to be noticed and seeks attention in inappropriate ways. You placed him on probation a year ago for public intoxication and selling a small amount of marijuana, ordering a 6-week stint in a drug education program. This time around, Joey was caught breaking windows at the local high school with two older boys. His probation officer has also informed you that merchants have been complaining about a local teenage shoplifting ring and he suspects Joey is one of the participants. Joey's dad is a single parent trying to raise Joey and his younger sister on a librarian's income.

Your choice seems simple enough. Lost Boys, Inc., a highly touted program of The Institute of Character Development, has been recommended to you by Joey's probation officer. You have made a few calls. While there is no solid empirical evidence, anecdotal accounts from a number of parents and the school principal suggest that the program may be a good fit for Joey. Unfortunately, Joey's dad doesn't agree and wants Joey to be placed on traditional probation again. Dave Martinez, who considers himself an agnostic, believes adamantly in the separation of church and state and doesn't want his son participating in a program he considers little more than a recruiting program for Christianity.

You have talked with Reverend Bobby Joe Simpson and checked his credentials. While it is true he doesn't have an academic degree in psychology or mental health, his seminary education did include some courses on pastoral counseling. Reverend Simpson claims his program is not religious but is more in keeping with the current "restorative justice" movement. Still, you can understand Dave Martinez's concerns after reading the Lost Boys brochure. The character development training includes concepts of confessing one's wrongdoings; making some form of restitution; seeking forgiveness from those one has wronged; and experiencing redemption through confession, restitution, and a new attitude of service to others. One other feature that troubles Dave Martinez is the footnote at the bottom of the brochure indicating that "while not required, religious and social support services are available to young men and women who request them."

You understand a parent's desire to raise his or her child according his or her own values. That said, this is the only option currently open to you besides traditional probation, and if Joey gets in trouble again, he could be sent to the regional juvenile prison. You will have to render your decision within the hour.

Questions for Discussion

How important should a parent's wishes be in a case like this? What might be some advantages and disadvantages in assigning Joey to the "character development" program? As a judge, you have limited choices. What should you do?

Case 7

Murder by Internet

You are the district attorney staring out the window at the rain and wondering what is the world coming to? A 17-year-old boy has just bullied his former girlfriend to the point of her taking her own life. What indeed, was the world coming to?

Assistant DA Mark Jones arrives, plops down in the chair facing your desk, and opens the case file he brought with him. "What a mess. Makes me wonder if we weren't better off with my grandmother's telephone party line and televisions with three or four channels to watch. Back then, folks sat down and thought about what they were doing. They took the time to actually write and mail letters to their friends and family. Now they tweet, snapchat, or text constantly—what they had for breakfast and whatever else catches their fleeting fancy. I was at a restaurant last night with my wife. The family at the next table never looked at or spoke to each other after they ordered. Four pairs of eyes were glued to their cell phones. They might as well have been eating alone."

"There you go, Mark, wanting to return to the good old days," you reply with a weary smile. "We live in the age of technology where people like you and me are moving in the slow lane. I have to admit there are some good things like cellphone videos that help apprehend criminals and help victims. And cameras that give us a better picture of what happens with our police officers when they make a traffic stop or arrest. Still . . ."

Mark pops a Nicorette in his mouth. "Yes, still . . . still the technology in the hands of immature teenagers is like giving a child a loaded shotgun or the keys to your car with no training or education regarding how use them or what the consequences might be if they are misused."

You look back at the rain falling outside and ask: "What's your opinion of what our response to this case should be?"

Mark folds his hands together. "The victim, Tami Green, had a history of depression—even attempted an overdose last year. She and Michael Eddy had been going steady the last three months, which according to her parents had perked her up. She seemed happier, less despondent."

"Until three weeks ago," you interject.

"That's right," Mark replies. "Three weeks ago, the couple broke up after an argument and Michael started spreading rumors about her sexuality and publicly disclosed Tami's history of depression on Facebook, while stating that she would never find a good boyfriend because she was 'crazy' and 'worthless.'" Mark rubs his chin and continues, "Michael's friends didn't help the situation by calling her ugly and commenting on her clothing choices."

You return your gaze to Mark. "You can't just blame Michael's friends. Even Tami's friends made inappropriate comments. The boys commented on how they would like to 'hook up' with her, and the girls made comments on how nice her breasts were and that she should have no problem finding another boyfriend that would overlook the rest of her body. They may have been trying to cheer her up, but this could have made her feel like just an object and further increased her depression. Unfortunately, we will never know."

Shaking his head, Mark replies, "Yep. The friends also looked the other way when Tami started posting memes on her Facebook wall indicating that she was thinking about taking her life. Everyone said that they thought Tami was just looking for attention, not seriously considering suicide."

Drumming your fingers on the desktop, you reply: "But Michael knew."

"That's right," Mark replied. "He did, indeed. And the clincher is we have a text from Tami that asked Michael if she could talk to him about her suicidal feelings, and Michael's reply was 'if you are looking for sympathy from me, you are looking in the wrong place. I don't care whether you live or die. Why don't you simply end it with a bullet to the head? That will be more effective than your previous suicide attempt.'"

You shake your head. "Now that Tami is gone the entire school is shocked and Michael says that he would have never responded in that way if he knew Tami would actually go through with it. Of course, all of Michael and Tami's friends are having similar reactions. But I think that we could convince a jury that Michael's actions, and maybe the comments of his friends, could rise to the level of manslaughter. What's your recommendation?"

Discussion Questions

In what ways have technological developments in communication helped and hurt individuals and families? What particular dangers does technology pose for younger children and for people suffering from emotional distress? Do you think that the DA should charge Michael or anyone else for their involvement in Tami's death? Can you think of anything that schools, families, and the criminal justice system could do that might help correct the excesses and destructive potential of texting and posts on social media?

Case 8

Where Does Protest End and Crime Begin?

The past few months have been the most difficult of your career, and it seems to be getting worse. As the district attorney for a relatively peaceful college town, your tenure had been mostly free of public controversy. However, that all changed two months ago when a police officer shot and killed an unarmed male student at the local university. The student fled on foot after being pulled over on a traffic stop, apparently because he had some drugs in his possession. After a short chase, the student turned toward the police officer and appeared to reach for something in his jacket. Fearing that this object might be a gun, the officer shot and killed the man. No gun was found; the student apparently had been reaching for the bag of drugs. The incident was caught on a cell phone video from a distance that made it difficult to determine exactly what happened. After spending two months examining the cell phone video and interviewing the officer, you had determined that there was not enough evidence to bring criminal charges against the police officer.

The backlash from your decision caught almost everyone in the law enforcement community off guard. The day after your decision was announced, an impromptu protest was organized by a large group of college students who believed that the local incident was yet another example of police brutality. Shortly before noon, 40 students walked out of their classes and marched to a crosswalk on the busy street in front of the university. They then linked arms along the crosswalk, effectively blocking all four lanes of traffic. After repeatedly telling the students to cease their protest and allow traffic to flow freely, the police officers began arresting each protester. At that point, the students began assaulting the police officers, who then retaliated by using pepper spray and tasers. Several onlookers videotaped the incident, which quickly became the focus of the evening newscast.

You are trying to determine how to proceed with criminal charges against the protesters when Gary Suttles, the police chief, enters your office. The police officers had charged each protester with disorderly conduct and resisting arrest, but you are unsure about the best path forward. Chief Suttles pushes you to proceed with the prosecution and points out that the video evidence is clear and that each case will result in a conviction. However, you are worried that pursuing this course might reinforce the already negative stereotype of the police department and the district attorney's office. Each of the protesting students had a clean criminal record, and the conviction would make it difficult for them to find a job after graduating. Your gut tells you that these are good kids that simply got caught up in a mob mentality during the protest. On the other hand, you could drop all charges and use this as a teaching moment for the students. This action might also result in negative public reaction or might even send a message that this type of behavior is acceptable in the future.

Discussion Questions

Should the district attorney use his discretion to drop the criminal charges against the college students? What would be the consequences of such an action? Are any compromises available that could restore the public's trust in the police and district attorney's office?

SECTION II

Rethinking Punishment

Corrections is assigned the task of carrying out the punishment levied, whether prison, jail, or sanctions served in the community. This section explores those topics. The eight cases allow you to relate to correctional situations from a variety of perspectives, including those of correctional employees and people in the community. For example, you will read about the minister who has a parishioner who is an ex-offender, the sheriff who is struggling to deal with the mental health needs of his inmates, and the probation officer deciding whether a young man deserves yet another chance.

Introduction

Change and reform in the American criminal justice system is a slow process. The manner in which criminals are apprehended, tried, convicted, and corrected has remained similar for nearly two centuries. Despite the increased push for evidence-based policies, policy makers must weigh the effectiveness of a new treatment in conjunction with political pressure, economics, and societal attitudes. Ultimately, a correctional reform can only be implemented effectively once it has received some level of community support. The community is also asked to actively assist the justice system in correcting deviant behavior. Whether this occurs within a correctional facility or in a community-based setting, citizens can help improve criminal behavior through education, employment, mental health care programs, and religious services.

The Role of the Community in Punishment

The role of the community in correctional programs depends largely on the interaction between the criminal justice system, political influences, and public attitudes. Typically, citizens respond to criminal activity by demanding greater action from the police and courts. For decades, the police sector has been promoting the concept of crime prevention to the public. The police have attempted, with some success, to educate the public regarding their responsibility in crime prevention and control. These responsibilities include techniques such as locking our cars at night and participating in neighborhood watch programs. The community also has an important role to play in the court system. Perhaps the most visible role involves our civic duty to participate in juries. However, the role of the crime victim is often overlooked. We know that many victims fail to report crime to the police or refuse to cooperate with the prosecution. Either of these actions can result in a failure to provide punishment and/or treatment to the offender and ultimately may undermine the community's crime prevention strategy. Thus, an effective justice system requires mutual trust between the community and the court system.

The correctional sector has also attempted to invite public participation. Although this endeavor has not been promoted on as grand a scale as crime prevention programs and civic responsibilities of jury duty, corrections has made some inroads. Citizen involvement in voluntary services, counseling centers, clinics, hotlines, vocational outreach, and so on are examples of these efforts.

The community has not always been viewed as a resource in addressing offender problems. For many years, the community was viewed only as harboring the causes of crime—the evil influences of bad company were viewed as the principal sources of criminal behavior. Removing the offender from a corrupting environment and confining him or her in a correctional institution eliminated temptation and provided the opportunity to change his or her ways through penitence, from which the term *penitentiary* was derived (Wodahl & Garland, 2009).

Many early community-based correctional efforts were criticized because they were contrary to the reform-through-isolation approach. It was believed that bringing ex-offenders together in halfway houses and group therapy was asking for trouble because they would inevitably revert to criminal behavior. Despite some progress in overcoming this view of crime, criminals, and the community, the attitude persists. For example, researchers found that the public was generally supportive of many initiatives designed to help reintegrate former offenders into society. However, this support decreased when residents were asked whether they would approve of programs such as transitional housing to be located in their neighborhood (Garland, Wodahl, & Schuhmann, 2013). The desire for offenders to be rehabilitated is accompanied by fears of being too close to the process. The reality is that the distinction between criminal and noncriminal is not as clear as many imagine, and most of us interact with those who have committed criminal acts on a daily basis. This section focuses on the role of the community in positively impacting offenders' lives at various levels of the justice system.

Incarceration

Approximately one-third of those who are supervised by the justice system are incarcerated in a jail or prison (Kaeble & Cowhig, 2018). The basic difference between a jail and a prison is that a prison utilizes correctional treatment programs and is intended for long-term incarceration, while a jail is intended to be used as a temporary detention center. The prison population increased by more than 400% from the early 1970s to 2009 before peaking at 1,615,487 and slowly declining. At year-end 2016, there were 1,505,397 people under the jurisdiction of state and federal correctional authorities (Carson, 2018).

Research generally finds that prison experiences increase recidivism among offenders. For example, one group of researchers found that prisoners had a significantly higher recidivism rate than a matched group of felons who had received probation (Mears, Cochran, & Bales, 2012). This should not be surprising. After all, the experience of imprisonment involves an offender being placed in a concrete cell where they associate with other criminals (Listwan, Sullivan, Agnew, Cullen, & Colvin, 2013). Of course, prison is needed for many offenders who have committed a serious crime or would otherwise pose a risk to society. More than half (54%) of prisoners are incarcerated for violent offenses, with murder, robbery, and rape/sexual assault being the most common categories (Carson, 2018).

A term of incarceration inside a state or federal prison strains the social relationships that an offender had with the community. Maintaining social ties is critically important to an inmate's chance of abstaining from crime once released from prison (Cobbina, Huebner, & Berg, 2012). One way to maintain these social ties is through prison visitation. Regular visits by family and friends have been shown to reduce the likelihood of recidivism (Duwe & Clark, 2011). However, the reality is that many inmates (especially those who have committed serious crimes or have a long history of criminal behavior) do not receive regular visitation from friends and family (Cochran, Mears, & Bales, 2017). Fortunately, prisoners often get visits from community volunteers such as pastors or others wishing to serve as mentors to the inmates. Visits from these volunteers significantly improved recidivism outcomes (Duwe & Johnson, 2016).

Prisons also rely on volunteers to assist in religious activities, job training, education classes, and various other types of training. Volunteers allow the prison to run more efficiently while providing offenders with the skills needed to succeed once they are released from prison. For some inmates, simply building a relationship with a volunteer who is able to provide encouragement and support may lead to positive change. Prison volunteers generally indicate that they enjoy their experiences and can sometimes tell a positive difference in inmate behavior over a period of time (Kort-Butler & Malone, 2015).

Prior to 1980, jail populations remained relatively stable. The midyear jail population peaked at 785,500 in 2007, which was the highest count since 1982 (Zeng, 2018). From 2011 to 2016, the population was again relatively stable. There were 740,700 jail prisoners at midyear 2016. Many county and regional jail facilities are paid through state funds to house state prisoners. There were 83,700 prisoners held in local jails in 2016 (Kaeble & Cowhig, 2018). The practice of holding state and federal prisoners in county facilities or local jails provides the local community additional revenues. It is usually cost effective to house 100 inmates as opposed to 50, since the increase in food and utility costs are only slightly higher. The practice allows state prisons to combat overcrowding by allowing less serious offenders to serve their sentences in local jails. The state is able to reduce the costs of building new prison facilities which, in turn, saves tax money. State prisoners housed in local jails are usually assigned a jail in close proximity to their homes. This allows for more frequent visitation from family members and support from their own community. However, many local communities, particularly in rural areas, began to rely on the revenue generated from the state inmates as well as the free labor which allowed local municipalities to hire fewer employees (Kang-Brown & Subramanian, 2017). The recent decline in the prison population has put significant economic pressure on many local jail budgets with fewer inmates are being sent to local facilities (Grim, 2016).

Many jails have incorporated correctional treatment programs formerly found only in prisons. Many counties have changed old workhouse jail systems into contemporary work-release programs. Under work-release programs, selected inmates are released from the jail during the day to work regular jobs in the community; they return to the jail at the conclusion of the workday. Previously such inmates might have performed workhouse chores such as cleaning the courthouse or washing police cars. Work-release programs allow inmates to develop their skills while gainfully employed. Recreational and educational programs in local jails have decreased the number of inmate assaults and staff-inmate conflicts by providing an outlet for cell-block boredom

(Wooldredge & Steiner, 2013). Community support and resource groups (YMCA, church groups, etc.) have contributed educational instruction and facilities as well as equipment to local jail inmates (e.g., weight lifting, ping-pong, video games, etc.).

The jail population increased with the deinstitutionalization of mentally ill patients that began in the 1960s. As mental hospitals closed across the country, jails witnessed a large increase in inmates with serious mental health conditions. Today, jails hold far more mentally ill individuals than mental hospitals. In fact, one survey of jail inmates showed that 44% had previously been told by a mental health professional that they had a mental disorder (Bronson & Berzofsky, 2017). These individuals are at increased risk for recidivism, victimization inside the jail, suicide, and disruptive behavior (Treatment Advocacy Center, 2014). It is clear that jails are not the most productive environments for mentally ill patients. Fortunately, improved training, education, and collaboration between mental health and corrections officials can improve the quality of life for these mentally ill individuals (Ellis & Alexander, 2017). However, communities across the country should be better educated to appreciate the implications of incarcerating mentally ill patients in jails for minor offenses (Kerle, 2016). Ultimately, substantial change will only occur once the public support exists for investments in community-based mental health services.

Parole

Parole is the supervision of offenders granted conditional release from prison by a parole board (Travis & Edwards, 2015). It is an executive-branch decision versus probation, which is a judicial decision, as discussed in section I. Parole releases inmates if the parole board decides incarceration has achieved its maximum benefit and that community-based guidance, counseling, and behavior monitoring will both assist the ex-offender in his or her attempt to avoid future crime and protect the community during the adjustment period. In 2016, there were 870,500 people on parole, an increase of 20% since 2000 (Kaeble & Cowhig, 2018). Parolees (13.2%) and jail inmates (11.2%) were the smallest shares of the correctional population versus 22.8% for prison and 55.5% for probation.

Prison overcrowding is one factor that has encouraged an increase in the use of parole (Bodenhorn, 2016). There are three essential elements of parole: (1) preparing inmates for release and developing pre-parole reports for prisoners; (2) conducting hearings regarding parole eligibility, granting parole, revoking parole, and terminating parole supervision; and (3) supervising parolees in the community. Inmates may also be released through the expiration of their sentence (flat-time) or through the accumulation of good-time credits.

Research shows that post-prison monitoring could be reduced for some offenders to direct limited resources toward those most likely to reoffend (Kappeler & Potter, 2018). The number of prisoners released after serving their full sentences has increased for several decades and now accounts for 1 in 5 releases (Rhine, Petersilia, & Reitz, 2015). Many of those ex-offenders need reentry services but do not receive them. Conversely, many low-risk offenders are paroled under post-release supervision when supervision is not necessary. Resources that could be better used elsewhere are wasted, and the parolees are at risk of reincarceration if they do not meet the supervision requirements.

Reentry

In 2016, the number of prisoners released back into the community was 2% lower than in 2015—626,000 versus 641,000 (Carson, 2018). Prisoners face a number of challenges while making the transition from prison to the communities. These individuals typically have low levels of education, substance abuse or mental health problems, few prospects for meaningful job opportunities, and difficulty finding housing. They often return to the same negative influences that contributed to their criminal behavior. Policy makers have increasingly focused on creating programs that aid prisoners in transitioning to life in the community.

Most contemporary models for prison reentry stress the importance of collaborating with community agencies to provide substance abuse treatment, financial assistance, mentoring services, and help repairing the damage to family relationships that have been negatively impacted by incarceration (Garland & Hass, 2015). California's governmental agencies are working with community-based organizations, faith-based communities, and families to ensure successful reentry to break the cycle of reincarceration (Ono, 2016). Outside organizations partner with in-prison and community programs to provide, for example, career technical education, substance abuse disorder treatment programs as well as a therapeutic arts program to help inmates express themselves. The executive director of the Los Angeles Regional Reentry Partnership commented that it is necessary for communities to challenge themselves rather than expecting the government to do everything. People return to their communities, their churches, and their families. Community-based organizations can create a welcoming environment for ex-offenders and help them become resources for the community.

Community-based organizations often have a limited number of paid staff and rely heavily on volunteers to provide their services (Willison, Brazzell, & Kim, 2011). In fact, these organizations likely could not exist without those in the community giving their time and talents to help prisoners reintegrate into society. Community volunteers are also needed to mentor released inmates. Volunteers provide services such as career advice; they also provide emotional support and serve as accountability partners (Umez, Cruz, Richey, & Albis, 2017). Ex-prisoners are sometimes solicited to serve as mentors. People released from prison face barriers to housing and employment and stigmatization because of their criminal records. They may doubt that they will be successful.

> Peer mentoring can offer a unique type of support that is not provided by other services or traditional mentoring practices. Because of their shared experiences of incarceration, peer mentors and participants can reach a level of understanding that would not otherwise be possible with mentors who do not have that experience. Participants might be more apt to trust and accept direction from peers who have lived through the incarceration and reentry process. (p. 10)

Peer mentors provide models that successful reentry is possible, thereby increasing motivation.

Those leaving a period of incarceration are expected to become productive, self- sustaining members of the community. Unfortunately, these offenders are usually subject to several financial obligations such as court costs, restitution to the victim, and costs associated with their treatment (Pogrebin, West-Smith, Walker, & Unnithan, 2014). As mentioned earlier, these offenders usually have limited levels of education, a lack of job skills, and a host of health problems that could impact their job search. As a result, obtaining meaningful employment serves as one of the largest challenges that ex-inmates face as they return to the communities. Successful reintegration requires employers who are willing to hire those with a criminal history. One study found that a little more than half of employers were willing to hire an ex-offender, but this willingness depended on the type of crime committed (Atkin & Armstrong, 2013). Not surprisingly, employers were more willing to hire offenders convicted of DUI or drug possession than those convicted of violent crimes.

It should be noted that employers also face barriers to hiring ex-offenders. First, many state laws prohibit offenders from working in certain job categories (Cantora, 2015). In addition, negligent hiring liability makes an employer civilly liable for the illegal conduct of an employee if the employee's conduct was foreseeable (Shepard, 2011). The act of hiring an individual with a criminal record could be construed as an indicator of foreseeable conduct if that employee commits a crime while on the job. This creates a dilemma for employers who wish to hire ex-offenders but also fear the legal liabilities of doing so.

Several states have taken steps to reduce or eliminate the liability created from hiring a person with a criminal background.

Community Corrections

The concept of community-based corrections grew from three basic issues: (1) increased concern over prison conditions, (2) the rising cost of incarceration, and (3) belief in the efficacy of rehabilitative programs (Wodahl & Garland, 2009). In 2016, the total population under community supervision (probation and parole) was 4,537,100 (Kaeble & Cowhig, 2018). About 7 in 10 persons under correction supervision were supervised in the community compared to 3 in 10 incarcerated in state or federal prisons.

The least punitive form of community corrections is diversion. Diversion typically involves an agreement with the court to avoid prosecution for minor offenses in exchange for good behavior or participation in a treatment program. More punitive forms of community corrections involve group homes, house arrest, and halfway houses. It should be noted that the mere operation of a group home or work-release center within the community is no guarantee that any meaningful ties with the local community will be established. In other words, a correctional program that happens to be located within a community does not necessarily meet the standards of community-based corrections, which include a philosophical commitment to the humane and effective treatment of offenders.

The 1970s witnessed phenomenal growth in community-based correctional programs. With federal assistance funds (e.g., LEAA), many communities funded programs that were poorly planned and/or implemented. When research began to demonstrate that community-based correctional strategies were often not very effective, program growth began to slow. Political conservatism and the economic recession of the 1980s also contributed to the decline in program growth. The loss of federal assistance plus political and economic factors in the last decade of the twentieth century and the first decade of the twenty-first resulted in attempts by many states and communities to develop innovative correctional programs. Victim restitution, community-service programs, electronic monitoring, and justice reinvestment are examples of programs implemented for community-based corrections.

Restitution and community-service programs are designed to restore what has been lost as a result of a crime. Monetary restitution programs provide financial payments from the offender to the crime victim. Although the concept of restitution has been around for centuries, it has often played an insignificant part in the criminal justice system. Traditionally, the state has been viewed as the injured party in a criminal offense. Community-service programs make restoration by requiring the offender to work in programs or on projects designed to enhance the public welfare (Latessa & Smith, 2015; Whitehead, Dodson, & Edwards, 2013). Community-service programs have been developed in an attempt to provide creative alternatives to monetary payments. Today, restitution and community-service programs are common alternatives or supplements to traditional dispositions, because they combine benefits to the offender, the victim, and the community.

Although restitution and community-service programs appear to be relatively simple responses to the crime problem, several legal and social issues have emerged with their use. The imposition of these punishments is often arbitrary; judges require restitution in some cases but not in others. Low-income or unemployed offenders struggle to pay for basic needs; making restitution is often impossible. Increased monitoring of meeting the imposed conditions widens the net of social control (Haynes, Cares, & Ruback, 2015; Sarnoff, 2014). In addition, some debate exists over whether those who fail to comply with these punishments should be incarcerated. These issues should be systematically addressed in any program attempting to use restitution or community service before implementation. Despite these issues, restitution and community-service programs have achieved the support of the community and criminal justice practitioners on the basis of their economic benefits to the victim and service benefits to the community.

Electronic monitoring was introduced in 1984 to relieve prison overcrowding and to provide a sanction more lenient than prison but more punitive than standard probation (Andersen & Andersen, 2014). The innovation was celebrated as the future of corrections for its potential for rehabilitation at a lower cost than imprisonment. By the late 1990s, electronic monitoring lost some of its appeal. Monitoring offenders was expensive; it facilitated putting more people under control of the criminal justice system, and technical violations returned many people to custody. Despite these problems, electronic monitoring alleviates some of the negative consequences of imprisonment. It facilitates the maintenance of family ties, allows the possibility for employment, reduces associations with criminal peers, and causes less stigma.

These systems use radio frequency (RF) technology (usually in the form of an ankle bracelet and a fixed receiver) or GPS tracking (a smart-phone device) to detect violations of the conditions of probation or parole. For example, GPS monitoring can be used to ensure that sex offenders do not enter certain restricted areas, such as schools or daycare facilities. This technology can also be used to help supervise those on house arrest. House arrest is a sentence imposed by the court in which the offenders are legally ordered to remain confined to their home. RF devices monitor presence in or absence from a fixed location.

While house arrest may be viewed by many as a less serious punishment compared to imprisonment, many offenders view electronic monitoring as punitive, controlling, and painful (Andersen & Andersen, 2014). Offenders generally pay $10 to $15 per day to be monitored (Karsten & West, 2017). Some courts base the fees on the user's ability to pay; in other jurisdictions, users are sent to jail for failure to pay the fees. The use of electronic monitoring more than doubled from 2005–2015 (Pew Charitable Trusts, 2016). Although electronic monitoring should not a considered a "silver bullet" that will enhance community safety (DeMichele, 2014), its use will likely continue to increase in the foreseeable future.

The pressure to divert offenders to community-based alternatives increases when budgets are strained during economic recessions. Justice reinvestment programs began with the goal of reducing the prison population and investing the monetary savings into increased education and revitalization of disadvantaged neighborhoods (Austin et al., 2013). These programs seem to have been successful at reducing incarceration in several states. However, the savings have not typically been directed at disadvantaged neighborhoods. Instead, the savings are most often focused on community-based corrections initiatives such as improved substance abuse and mental health treatment, transitional housing, and victim's services (LaVigne et al., 2014).

The use of volunteers in community corrections permit criminal justice agencies to make better use of professional staff, individualize services to offenders, and increase public awareness of correctional programs, problems, and issues. While some improvement in the use of volunteers is needed, any drawbacks are outweighed by the usefulness of volunteer services in community corrections. Areas of improvement for volunteers in community corrections include recruitment, training, and government support. Many states are exemplary in that they require volunteers to undergo the same training and qualifications as regular staff.

Community corrections offers a revised way of thinking about punishment. Prior to 1973, there was also a belief in rehabilitation as an appropriate response to criminal behavior, but the pendulum began swinging to more punitive attitudes. The solution to deterring crime was to enact harsh sentencing and to remove criminals from society (Kappeler & Potter, 2018). At that time, less than 0.2% of the U.S. population was incarcerated, similar to the rest of the developed world. Today the number of people imprisoned in the United States is five times the average for similar industrialized nations. Criminologists have labeled the increased punitiveness in the treatment of prisoners after 1973 as *penal harm*. The supermax facility and solitary confinement were direct outgrowths of punitive ideology.

The collateral effects of incarceration are devastating. "Every person incarcerated represents a family dismantled. Every parent locked up is a child who grows up visiting a prison with limited interaction with a parent" (Shapiro, 2017, p. 15). Corrections in the community alleviates some of the collateral effects but requires constant vigilance. If ex-offenders fail to reintegrate, they are not the only ones who suffer; much of society is impacted by the consequences of mass incarceration and the loss of human and social capital. "Every year there is an exponential impact as valuable lives are wasted, communities are strained, the public is less safe, and dreams are deferred" (Martin, 2012, p. 49).

Summary

Traditionally, correctional programs have operated in out-of-sight prisons and other custodial facilities. The concept of community-based corrections grew from three basic issues: (1) increased concern over prison conditions, (2) the rising cost of incarceration, and (3) belief in the efficacy of correctional treatment/rehabilitation. Community corrections provides meaningful ties between offenders and their local community. The development and maintenance of a successful community correctional program relies on a balance between public attitudes, the criminal justice system, and related systems (e.g., education, employment, housing, etc.).

The role of the community in correctional programs depends to a large extent on the interaction between the criminal justice system, political influences, and public attitudes. Community involvement in corrections has typically been seen primarily in reentry or community corrections programs, though citizens are often also able to engage with incarcerated offenders. Many volunteers are motivated by religious factors and volunteer for a specific religious service or faith-based nonprofit community organizations. These organizations can be particularly helpful for providing prisoner reentry services. Although people may be concerned with the religious basis of such organizations, research has shown that spreading religion is not usually the primary goal of such organizations (Denney & Tewksbury, 2013, Duwe & King, 2012; Kerley & Copes, 2008). Rather, these organizations provide offenders with benefits such as emotional support, education, and employment assistance. Ultimately, community assistance facilitates successful rehabilitation and reentry.

Case 1

The Minister and
the Ex-Offender

As one of your community's leading ministers, you have always spoken out for progressive correctional reform. Your congregation has usually backed you. On the few occasions when they did not, they still remained tolerant of your views. Now, however, things are different. Sally, a former member of your church, was once active in working with the church youth. Convicted of embezzling funds from the local bank where she worked, she was sentenced to a year in prison. As her minister, you kept in contact with her from the beginning of her imprisonment.

Everyone has financial burdens at one time or another, and Sally had experienced a succession of problems. The clincher was her husband's permanent disability as a result of an accident. The bills began to pile up faster than she could pay them. They had mortgaged their house and sold one of their two cars. Finally, in desperation, Sally "borrowed" several thousand dollars from the bank where she had worked as a teller for years. When her crime was discovered, her world crumbled.

She has now returned to the community after serving her prison term. When you talked to her the day after she returned, you realized that she was a broken woman. Her daughter had dropped out of school to care for her father, and his disability check was their primary source of income. You counseled her and encouraged her to try to regain her place in the community. You also helped her find work and even suggested that she return to your church, where she had previously been very active. She was reluctant to rejoin the church, fearing rejection by the congregation. You tried to reassure her that everyone was behind her and wanted her to return to the church. In fact, some members had told you they were sympathetic. When you learned that there would soon be an opening in the Sunday school for a youth director, you asked Sally to consider taking the position. After several days of thinking about it, she agreed.

You brought her name before the Sunday school committee; all of the members refused to consider her for the youth leader position. Their attitude took you totally by surprise. Their words remain all too clear in your mind: "How would it look to the rest of the community to have an ex-convict directing our youth?" Should you fight for what you believe is right and risk dissension, or should you tell Sally that her fears are more valid than you had thought—that her former fellow church members have not been able to forgive and forget?

Questions for Discussion

In this particular case you, as the minister, must make a difficult decision. If you insist on Sally being allowed to become a youth leader and the dissenting members relent, what kind of emotional pressure would this put on Sally, and how would she handle it? On the other hand, if you "give in" to the disagreeable committee members and inform Sally of their decision, what impact will your action have on Sally's and your own self-concept, as well as your leadership ability in the church? Perhaps you were not fully aware of the church's true attitude concerning Sally as an ex-offender. What could you have done to become more aware of their feelings?

Case 2

See No Evil, Hear No Evil

You are an assistant district attorney for a small, rural county in the South. You were hired straight out of law school and have been on the job for three years. You have formed good working relationships with the other prosecutors, most of the town's private attorneys, and, perhaps most importantly, the local judges. You have worked hard to foster these professional relationships, as experience has taught you that the rapport you have with someone can often be the difference in a motion or a case going your way.

As part of your job, several times a week—and sometimes several times a day, you are forced to dismiss domestic violence charges against someone because the victim refuses to testify. In many cases you find this unwillingness to assist the court unfortunate but understandable. The victim often lives with, has children with, or is financially dependent on the abuser. From the victim's perspective, the fear and the unwillingness to cooperate with you in the prosecution of their partner is reasonable. If the abuser is convicted and sentenced, what will the abuser do when released? Will the abuse become worse? If the victim's spouse is incarcerated for any length of time, who will pay the rent? Purchase the groceries? Watch the children when it is necessary to be away from home?

Sometimes, the victim did not call the police and views the arrest and subsequent criminal charges against her or his partner as an intrusion into their domestic affairs. You have seen numerous explanations of why a domestic violence victim might not want to appear in court and testify against the defendant. Though these scenarios are unfortunate, they are the realities that many domestic violence victims must deal with every day.

The judge in the General Sessions Court to which you are assigned has decided that he is tired of dismissing cases because of uncooperative witnesses. The judge believes that failure to testify wastes the time and money of the police department, the county jail, and the court system. The judge is not indifferent to the plight of domestic violence victims, but he has grown frustrated with releasing abusers back into society—often the same offender multiple times. Several days ago, after a particularly busy docket in which he was forced to dismiss the charges against a half-dozen domestic violence defendants because their victims did not appear to testify, the judge had had enough. This morning in open court before hearing any cases, the judge decreed that any domestic violence victim who either did not appear in court after being served a summons or who refused to testify to the facts once on the witness stand would be held in contempt of court and ordered to serve time in the county jail. The judge thought that this would help solve the problem of uncooperative domestic violence victims; but you immediately saw the truth of the situation. The judge's order would put the district attorneys' office in an unenviable position. Incarcerating the victim of an offense for failure to testify would victimize that person even further—and would most likely lead to more victims being afraid to report abuse. In addition, the local press would vilify the participation of any court officials in carrying out the judge's decree.

By the noon recess that day, the judge had ordered the jailing of 2 women for 7 days for contempt of court: one for failing to appear in court and the other for refusing to assist the DA's office in the prosecution of her husband for domestic violence. The judge asked you to come to his chambers during the recess. When you arrived in his office, the judge wasted no time in telling you he thought his strategy was off to a great start. You felt otherwise. Beaming with pride, the judge asked you what you thought about the results of his new policy: you hesitated while you collected your thoughts.

For the first time since you began your career, you find yourself in a difficult situation, and you can see no options that lead to a happy ending. If you tell the judge the truth—that you think his new policy is harmful, ill-advised, and counterproductive—there is no telling how he will take your candor. Will he take it in stride, or will he resent your honesty and punish you for it in the courtroom as a means of nursing his wounded pride? If you lie to him and tell him the new contempt policy is wonderful, you will be aiding in the unnecessary suffering of countless victims of domestic violence, as well as complicating your own job by giving those victims even more reasons to hesitate to report abuse to the police. No matter what choice you make, somebody is going to suffer. The only question is: will it be you or someone else?

Questions for Discussion

As the assistant district attorney, you are not only responsible for your actions within the courtroom but are also held to a high standard by the public. If you do not tell the judge that you think his policy is harmful, how will you account to the public for the court's decision to punish domestic violence victims for their lack of cooperation? Do you feel it is your job as the assistant district attorney to defend the decision of a judge who works in the same courtroom?

Case 3

Corrections in Jail
Mental Health vs. Custody

Following a long tenure in the Federal Bureau of Investigation, you returned to your rural hometown and were elected sheriff. Your campaign pledge was for ethical and financial responsibility in the sheriff's office. This message was well received due to the previous sheriff's conviction in a bribery scheme and his constant requests for increases in the sheriff's budget.

Having been on the job for 6 months, you find that your campaign promises might be more difficult to uphold than you originally thought. One particular area of concern involves your observation of the county jail operations. It seems that the same offenders continue to be booked into the jail on petty charges and then released on bail shortly thereafter. After talking to the jail intake officers and your sheriff's deputies, it becomes clear to you that many of these offenders have an underlying mental health issue that causes them to commit a low-level crime or to be involved in domestic disputes that often involve a relative calling the police. In fact, medical records indicate that approximately 35% of the jail inmates have previously received mental health treatment.

You begin to feel that the sheriff's department can do a better job at intervening both before and after these mentally ill suspects are arrested. With assistance from your staff, you draft a proposal to provide improved training to your deputies and correctional officers to identify arrestees with mental illnesses. The hope is that the deputies can divert some of these mentally ill suspects into treatment programs instead of bringing them to the jail. Still, you realize that many suspects with mental illness will ultimately end up in the jail. For these cases, you propose a special unit within the jail to provide treatment and rehabilitation. The cost associated with the improved training, increased staffing, and facility upgrades is estimated at approximately $300,000 per year. However, you feel strongly that this is morally the correct course of action and also that it will save the county money in the long run by helping treat the underlying mental health issues.

Feeling confident, you propose these ideas at the next county commission meeting. The commission unanimously criticizes your plan and expresses disappointment that they are hearing yet another request for increased funding from the sheriff's department. The mayor pointedly tells you to "worry about running your department instead of running a psych ward. Your department historically has just been a black hole where we throw money but never see any results." Other commissioners suggest that you could find other ways to save money to offset the costs of the proposal but that no additional money would be allocated to the sheriff's department.

You feel trapped by the commission's decision. In your mind, this proposal fulfills both of your campaign promises while helping the citizens of your hometown. Now, you face the prospect of helplessly watching the same people cycle through your jail without addressing their mental health needs. It is frustrating that the county commission cannot see the long-term success that this program would bring. Even so, you do understand that the trust between the sheriff's department and county leaders is strained due to the previous sheriff's mismanagement.

Questions for Discussion

In this situation, would you take the advice of the commission and "worry about running your department" or would you develop a new course of action that would not demand as many resources? If so, what would this new course of action consist of, and how would it be implemented? Are there any other agencies or institutions outside the criminal justice system that could provide assistance? How would you attempt to integrate these agencies, and would their participation affect the estimated cost of your proposal?

Case 4

A Family of Offenders

Jake is 13 years old, a little small for his age, yet streetwise and hardened. Jake's delinquent behaviors disqualified him from detention in a foster home or a group home, so he was committed to the state juvenile training school on three occasions. His commitments did not seem to have any effect on his subsequent conduct, except that his grades improved. Since being assigned as a juvenile aftercare worker in the county youth court, you have already seen Jake on several occasions and have heard many stories about his family, which your counterpart in the adult court calls "a breeding ground for felons." If Jake's early conduct is any indication, he will likely follow in his family's footsteps of criminal behavior. You decided to visit Jake's home to talk to his mother. Six of Jake's eight brothers and sisters have served jail sentences, and two brothers are presently in the state penitentiary. Sam, the oldest, is 22 and is serving eight years for armed robbery. Richard, age 19, is serving 20 years for the kidnapping and attempted rape of a high school girl who was walking home from school. Jake's two sisters, ages 17 and 18, have long records of shoplifting. The older one was involved in a killing at a local lounge and may be indicted at the next grand jury term.

The specific reason you decide to visit Jake's mother is that he has been associating with a group of four older boys (two of whom are believed to be his brothers) thought to be involved in a series of local robberies. The robbers always leave the scene on foot. On one occasion, a member, acting as a lookout, ran up to the three who were committing the robbery to warn them of an approaching car. Although identification was incomplete, a composite sketch indicated that Jake was the lookout. The rest of the gang was wearing stocking masks.

Jake's family lives in a three-room flat in the ghetto. Mattresses crisscross the floor of the common bedroom, and there is a new large screen television, "a gift from a friend," according to the mother. The third room appears to be the mother's private bedroom. The house is dirty, and the furniture in the main room gives the impression of a waiting room. The mother appears to be in business for herself, leaving any children remaining at home to take care of themselves. You doubt that your talk with Jake's mother will produce anything except evasiveness and hostility.

Jake's mother, obviously just out of bed for your 1:00 PM appointment, denies any possibility that Jake could be in any trouble, or even heading for trouble. She finally admits that Jake had been in trouble "once or twice" and then becomes belligerent, blaming the police for her son's trouble. She angrily tells you to "get out and don't come back."

About a month later, Jake and his brothers were arrested by a police officer who witnessed the group's latest robbery. The juvenile court waived jurisdiction, and Jake was sent to adult court. Although the court-appointed defense attorney attempted to have Jake tried separately, he and his brothers were tried together, and all were sentenced to a term of five years imprisonment. Because of his youth, Jake's sentence was suspended. You are asked by the adult probation supervisor to help with Jake's supervision (both adult and juvenile probation functions are integrated under the same authority in your state). Although Jake is legally bound to serve an adult's sentence and is responsible to the adult court, you may hold the key to his eventual rehabilitation, or there may be no such key. You want to salvage Jake from a career of crime, but the odds do not look good. Is there anything you can do, or should you just write Jake off?

Questions for Discussion

Jake seems to be moving toward crime as a career. Could Jake be removed from his toxic environment? Where could he be sent? What would be the consequences of such action on Jake and his family? Are there other alternatives?

Case 5

The Teacher, the Delinquent, and the Gang

Schools have certainly changed since you last taught in the classroom. It used to be short hair, no jeans, no slacks, and no fun! One of the reasons students looked forward to college was that they could do and dress as they pleased. But now, high schools are becoming very similar to college in many respects. Such traditional concepts as study hall and homeroom are beginning to disappear. Many high schools allow students much more flexibility in choosing the courses they take. You remember well how much you hated the prescribed schedules in your school system. Not only are students now allowed more freedom in choosing courses, but teachers are also allowed more freedom in experimenting with different teaching methods.

With a newly earned master of education degree, you have a number of ideas on how to improve the quality and interest of classroom instruction. Yet, as a 56-year-old teacher who hasn't taught in more than 25 years, you have some qualms. Your husband, a retired city engineer, cautioned you not to expect too much too soon; nevertheless, you remain optimistic about the possibilities of innovative educational techniques.

You found out quickly that some of the changes in contemporary high schools might not have been for the better. When you taught high school, the teacher was considered "boss," and his or her word was usually law. For those few students who did not accept it, detention and the threat of possible expulsion was usually enough to convince them. Now, however, student discipline seems weak, if it exists at all. In fact, your school principal, who believes in strict discipline, has been brought to court twice over being too punitive. Because the judge in your community also believes in strict discipline, the principal won both cases. However, student behavior has continued to become more aggressive, including several recent physical assaults on teachers. To make matters worse, several student groups are beginning to look more and more like gangs.

There appear to be three primary gangs vying for attention. The Rosewood Brothers took their name from a recent popular film; the group includes about a dozen young African American males ranging in age from 14 to 18. The Border Runners are young Latino males; the group also has about 12 members, ages 15 to 16. The Invisible Empire is a smaller group consisting of about five or six underachieving white male students. With their shaven heads, they look like skinhead "wannabes." There are girls who affiliate with each gang. Other than several fist fights and petty acts of vandalism, there have been no major confrontations. Recently, several members of the Invisible Empire boasted about getting their hands on two AK-47s. Mr. Smith, the principal of your school, seems a little nervous but hopes that several key graduations will take away the leadership of the gangs in question. You aren't so sure.

Against this backdrop, you are currently faced with a significant discipline problem in one of your own classes. A 15-year-old female student has consistently refused to cooperate with you regarding course assignments and behavior in the classroom. She hangs around with the Border Runners. At times she is belligerent, and at other times she simply ignores you. And every so often—just often enough to give you a faint sense of hope—she contributes something creative and positive to a class discussion. Unfortunately, just as quickly, she reverts to a rebellious act. Needless to say, such behavior encourages other members of the class to be disruptive also. In addition, several members of the Border Runners in your class occasionally encourage her to be disruptive.

This particular student has been in trouble with the police since she was 10 years old for truancy, occasional shoplifting, and minor vandalism. You have heard that the juvenile court judge has indicated that one more incident will result in her being adjudicated to confinement. The principal has agreed to have her expelled from school; expulsion would probably result in confinement in a juvenile facility.

You are uncertain as to what course of action to take. You would hate to see the student expelled, particularly given the probability that she would then enter the juvenile justice system. But you can accomplish very little in class as long as she continues to misbehave. You have tried to contact her parents, but they do not respond to your personal notes or your phone calls. Her affiliation with the Border Runners, as well as the larger issue of the emergence of the gangs themselves, concerns you. Something needs to be done, but what?

Questions for Discussion

Are you responsible only as a teacher, or do you also have responsibilities as a concerned citizen? What are community attitudes about expulsion? What other social agencies or nonprofit organizations might be helpful in this particular situation? Could you work with local law enforcement officials to address the emerging problems at the school without contributing to the school to prison pipeline?

Case 6

A Farmer's Dilemma

The crowd at Maybelle's Diner had thinned out by 10 o'clock. Two grizzled regulars with weather-worn skin from a lifetime of farming in the hot Texas sun sat in the rear of the diner next to the juke box. Ernest Tubb sang his classic country heart out as the retirees nodded their approval. The one wearing the greasy CAT hat took the toothpick out of his mouth. "Thank God Maybelle's kept this old jukebox going. As long as I've got a pocketful of quarters, real country singers like Hank and Ernest will keep on singing." His compadre chuckled. "Better your quarters than mine. Sooner or later this ol' jukebox like the three of us will be put out to pasture."

The front door of the diner opened, and Morris Townsend walked in. Maybelle looked up from her paperwork. "Morning, Sheriff. Bernie McCallister and Red Evans are waiting for you in the back dining room. You want anything?"

Morris took off his hat and wiped the sweat from his brow. "And a good morning to you, Miss Maybelle. A cup of your finest coffee will do." Sheriff Townsend pulled out a chair and sat down, looking at two of the county's biggest farmers sitting across from him. "What are you two up to?" he asked with a smile.

Red laughed as the Sheriff took the cup of coffee from the waitress. "No good, as usual."

Taking a sip, he looked at his two friends. "I know that's the truth. Speaking of the truth, why are we meeting this late in the morning in the back room at Maybelle's?"

Bernie folded his hands together on the table. "Morris, we have a big problem. Our crops are coming in and we don't enough people to work the fields."

Red Evans took off his cap and laid it on the table. "When they passed this new illegal immigration law, they didn't think about how it impacts us farmers. Better than half of our field workers are in jail awaiting deportation and a bunch more are afraid to show up."

"Last time folks came to work, ICE agents arrested them," Bernie chimed in. "Don't know if you read about it, but a couple of years ago in Alabama, crops rotted in the fields 'cause there was no one to harvest them."

Sheriff Townsend took another swallow of coffee and set his cup on the table. "Boys you know as well as I do, the law's the law. I don't make the laws. All I can do is try to enforce them."

"Maybe so, Morris, but if we lose those crops, our farming operations will be in jeopardy. And if things go south because of it, folks who are affected won't blame whatever numbskulls came up with a law without thinking it through, they'll blame us and you. Anyway, we aren't the only farmers affected by this situation. Most of the smaller farms also depend on the same field workers to help them out during harvest time."

The Sheriff looked at the two men sitting across from him. "I understand your problem, fellows, but don't see anything I can do about it."

Red looked at Bernie then back at the Sheriff. "How about putting those workers you have in the county jail on some kind of work release so they can help us out? The ICE agents are focusing on the western part of the state right now so maybe we can talk to the workers who are laying low to come to work as well."

"Let me get this straight," the Sheriff replied. "You want me to look the other way on the illegals still out and about and on top of that, set up some type of community corrections work release program for those folks who are currently in jail?"

Red Evans drummed his fingers on the table. "That's about the size of it. We hate to put you in this spot, but we don't know what else to do. No workers, no crops and no crops, a lot of unhappy folks who live here."

Morris Townsend stared at the ceiling as he thought about his friends' request. "You present a dicey proposition—one that may or may not work. I'll have to give it some thought and get back to you."

"That's all we ask, Morris. Just remember, time is short," Red replied.

As the Sheriff rose from the table, he offered his two friends a forlorn smile. "Human nature being what it is, I can't help but notice that no concerns have been voiced on behalf of the workers needed to bring in the crops. We all know what most likely will happen to them once the harvesting is finished."

Bernie gestured with his hands. "We feel bad for them, but we have to have our priorities."

Straightening his hat, Morris Townsend looked at his watch. "No doubt you do."

Questions for Discussion

What do you think the Sheriff should do? Should his priority be to enforce the letter and intent of the law or to try to help his two friends and the other farmers that the community depends on? What are some possible negative consequences for the Sheriff and farmers if their proposed plan doesn't work? What about the illegal immigrants? What should the outcome—legal and moral—be for them? What will the outcome most likely be? How does this case demonstrate the collateral effects of passing laws and creating enforcement policies that hurt the needs of the community?

Case 7

Revocation or
Yet Another Chance?

The court has sentenced Tommy Smith, age 21, for the second time in three years. The first conviction was for unlawful possession of marijuana. When Tommy's mother testified that he was needed to help support the family, the judge suspended the confinement and ordered Tommy to 6 months' probation. He was ordered to report to you, a state probation officer for the sixth judicial district, as you deemed necessary for his restoration to the community as a productive member. The probation period went well, and the court expunged the record.

Tommy has now been charged with breaking and entering, a lower degree of burglary in your state. The judge was somewhat exasperated but the expungement of the marijuana conviction meant that the breaking and entering was officially a first offense. The judge again suspended Tommy's sentence and ordered him to serve four years of supervised probation and to make restitution for the value of the items stolen. You felt that the term was somewhat severe, but you know that male offenders in Tommy's age range usually need a great deal of supervision and typically have a higher probability for repetitive criminal behavior than some other groups. In addition, recidivism for burglary is generally high.

The presentence investigation indicated that Tommy was 15 years old when his father disappeared. Soon after the disappearance, Tommy dropped out of high school to take a a job to help support his mother and his four brothers and sisters. Tommy had no juvenile record. He lives at home in a very small, well-kept apartment in a government-subsidized housing project. Tommy is no longer the only income provider. Two of his younger brothers both have decent-paying jobs and help support the family. One is an assistant manager at a fast-food restaurant, and the other is a plumber's apprentice.

You first interview Tommy and his job foreman. Tommy's foreman assures you that Tommy is a good worker. Despite Tommy's long absence from the job while in jail awaiting trial, the foreman would readily take Tommy back. Tommy also seemed to have a good relationship with his coworkers. Next you interview Tommy's mother. You want to capitalize on the strong mother-son relationship as an aid in reinforcing a responsible behavioral pattern, especially concerning Tommy's after-hours activities. Tommy's mother blames her son's criminal activity on his recent association with a bad crowd in the neighborhood.

The weekly consultations with Tommy and his mother appeared to be helping him meet the conditions of his probation with only minimal difficulty. Unfortunately, his love of excitement and the easy money to be gained with his new associates worked against his rehabilitation. He appeared on the court docket 12 months later for conspiracy and burglary of a railway freight car.

After noting a huge rise in rail cargo theft, the railway police had employed extra security officers to stop the gangs looting the boxcars. Tommy was caught on a Saturday night with three friends after breaking into five boxcars. Although nothing was missing from the boxcars, Tommy eventually admitted his intent to steal and implicated his companions in a similar manner. Because of Tommy's cooperation during the investigation, the district attorney decided not to prosecute the case against Tommy.

Now you must decide whether to initiate a revocation hearing. Tommy is a personable young man who just can't seem to say no to the influence of his friends after hours. You could revoke his probation or try another option: house arrest. If you placed him on house arrest during evenings for 6 months, he might find some new, less trouble-prone friends. You know from experience that house arrest doesn't work for everyone. However, with the strong support of Tommy's mother and his family, house arrest just might work in his case. In a sense, his probation deserves to be revoked. Yet, serving time in jail or prison seems unlikely to benefit him or society. The judge has deferred to your good judgment.

Questions for Discussion

Tommy has been diverted from the criminal justice system three times. Should there be a limit to the number of diversions? If the media reports the story, what public attitudes would you predict? Would sentencing Tommy to jail or prison deter criminal activity in the future? Is electronic monitoring an effective alternative? What are the potential benefits? Are there community resources that could help Tommy learn to reject associations that lead to criminal behavior?

Case 8

Peer Mentoring–Benefit or Bureaucratic Morass?

For the past 5 years, you have been the director of a human resources agency located in a rural area. One of the services that your agency provides is a reentry program for offenders who are returning to your community following a period of incarceration. During your tenure, you have focused most attention on meeting offenders' basic needs: housing, transportation, food, and employment. You visit with each offender approximately 6 months prior to release in order to introduce your agency's services and assess their needs. Following this meeting, you work closely with the state parole office to coordinate regular post-release meetings with the offender and identify other underlying issues such as substance abuse, mental health needs, or damaged family relationships, which may disrupt their successful reentry. Overall, you are satisfied with the connections that you have made within the community and are optimistic about your agency's ability to bridge the gap between the offender and the community. However, you continue to be frustrated that many offenders do not seem interested in taking advantage of your services.

Last month, your state announced the availability of a grant to help fund community-based offender peer-mentoring programs. The grant also funds a state-sponsored training where peer mentors can attend a 2-day class to become a certified peer specialist and a certified substance abuse counselor. While this training is optional, the grant does provide a modest stipend for those who attend. This is exciting news, as you hope that peer mentors will be able to reach your clients more effectively than your current staff is able to accomplish. Specifically, you hope that recruiting former offenders who have successfully integrated into the community using your agency will provide legitimacy to your services and motivate your clients to take advantage of these resources.

As you prepare to implement the peer-mentoring program, several unexpected barriers have emerged. First, recruiting mentors to participate in the program has been more difficult than you had imagined. Most of the potential mentors that you have reached out to feel that they do not have adequate skills to assist others. You have been reluctant to send prospective peer mentors to your state's certification program, preferring to train the mentors in house. Your main goal is to have your former clients reach out to new clients and describe the benefits of your program's services. You feel that the former clients are already familiar with your services and that the state's training might undermine some of what you would prefer the peers' message to be. Other prospective mentors have also expressed concern for the time that they might miss from work and their families.

Several institutional rules also complicate the adoption of a peer-mentoring program. For example, the local prison has a regulation restricting those with a criminal record from visiting current inmates. The prison can waive this policy on a case-by-case basis for inmates' immediate family members, but so far the administration has signaled that they would not waive their requirement for your agency's proposed peer mentoring program. This rule interferes with your original plan to begin the peer-mentoring process during the final few weeks of an offender's incarceration. Finally, you learn of a rule restricting parolees from intentionally associating with those who have been previously convicted of violent or sex offenses. This would significantly limit the program's scope, as your experience shows that violent or sex offenses are the very clients who would benefit most from a peer mentor. You begin to wonder whether the peer-mentoring program is worth the hassle.

Questions for Discussion

Does the director's reluctance to send potential peer mentors to the recommended state training undermine the program's potential effectiveness? Does the director appear to be most concerned with the offender or with her own agency? Should the state restrict the grant money to only those agencies that require the peer-mentor certification? Could the state have better coordinated the grant availability with the institutional and community corrections agencies? What would your next steps be?

SECTION III

The Inmate

In this section, the introduction and eight cases explore the world of inmates in prison. All types of persons are present in an inmate population; there are good and bad persons—some who feel a great deal of remorse for their offenses and others who seem to feel no remorse for their crimes. Bullies, drug abusers and embezzlers, as well as former school teachers, lawyers, and doctors comprise the typical prison population. To gain maximum understanding of the inmate in prison, you should attempt to relate to each case as if you were the inmate who is described. Potential solutions to the problems raised will be influenced by your ability to assess the information from multiple perspectives.

Introduction

Over two million Americans are incarcerated in either jails or prisons (Kaeble & Cowhig, 2018). Jail stays are generally for short periods of time—sometimes while the accused awaits court dates; other times after conviction for a misdemeanor offense. The weekly turnover rate of the nation's jail population is almost 55% (Zeng, 2018). In contrast, prison sentences are often for significant periods of time, sometimes for the rest of one's life. As a result, most research involving the effects of imprisonment has focused on prison sentences. In addition, most research has been about male prisoners, even though females are the fastest growing prison population group (Swavola, Riley, & Subramanian, 2016). The available information does suggest that female inmates have, in many respects, a much different experience than their male counterparts.

A better understanding of prison life is essential for anyone wishing to work in the corrections field. Although criminals differ on their perception of how "hard" prison life will be (Crank & Brezina, 2013), incarceration is, at the very least, a significant change in one's daily life. Prisons are total institutions where every aspect of life is controlled (Goffman, 1961). All activities—sleeping, eating, working, and leisure activities—are performed at the prescribed time in the same place with the same people (Whitehead, Dodson, & Edwards, 2013). The restriction on social interactions and lack of freedom makes prison life fundamentally different from life outside the prison and can have lasting impacts for inmates when they return to society.

Inmate Classification

Offenders are one of the most stigmatized groups in society. Stigma exists on three levels. At the structural level, laws and policies restrict ex-offenders from certain types of housing, employment, and voting. At the social level, the public, as well as correctional personnel, may have stigmatizing attitudes that discriminate against offenders. At the self-level, the individual can internalize stigma and feel devalued. The stigma attaches from the initial incarceration through post-release experiences (Moore, Stuewig, & Tangney, 2013).

Once an inmate is remanded to the custody of a correctional facility, he or she will be formally classified to determine the proper security level. Those assigned to a lower security level are typically allowed much more freedom to move around the facility and socialize with other inmates as compared to those assigned to high security levels. One study found that prisoners assigned to high custody levels were more likely to engage in prison misconduct, even after controlling for other institutional and individual-level predictors of misconduct (Worrall & Morris, 2011). Thus, while the institution assigns a security level that reflects the potential risk of an inmate engaging in misbehavior, the fact of labeling the offender can contribute to why an inmate misbehaves. Available treatment options might also vary depending on one's custody level. It is imperative that the prison classify inmates into security levels that accurately reflect the risks for the institution as well as the needs of the inmate.

Inmate classification processes have evolved as evidence-based tools have become available. The traditional classification process includes a number of areas: security concerns, physical health status, a psychological profile, vocational needs and job-related skills, and educational level. This process requires medical and related health examinations; psychological, educational, and vocational testing; and caseworker reviews. Correctional staff then make a classification decision based upon the results of the inmate's profile. The following sample case summary is a general example of the results of the inmate classification procedure.

Case Summary: John Doe—38767

Current Legal Status: Convicted 5–8–2017 of armed robbery. Serving 10–20 years. One prior conviction (4–26–1998) for burglary. Successfully completed probation.

Physical Health: Medical examination indicates no current problems, although past history of high blood pressure is noted. Dental examination reveals minor gum infection that can be treated effectively at the institutional dental clinic.

Psychological Profile: Psychological testing reveals client is currently experiencing mild depression, probably as a result of his recent imprisonment. No suicidal tendencies are indicated. Test results also suggest the potential for the client to be highly manipulative.

Educational Level: Educational testing indicates client is functioning at a 10th grade level.

Vocational Skills: Client has worked as a construction laborer and carpenter's helper.

Recommendation: Maximum security classification for the first 6 months, reduced to medium after that period of time, contingent on a review of the client's record. The client should also be encouraged to enroll in the G.E.D. preparation program. Client should be considered for a work assignment on the new prison gym construction project.

Contemporary prison classifications are often made with the assistance of a quantitative risk and need assessment tool. These assessments assign points based on several risk factors which have been shown to be associated with criminal behavior. These risk factors include static factors (e.g., offender's age, past involvement in criminal behavior) that do not change with treatment and dynamic factors (e.g., personality issues, problems with substance abuse) that can change with treatment. Higher scores on the risk assessment tools often correspond to closer supervision in the prison setting (Sun, 2013). Inmate classification is a process that typically begins upon the offender's entry into the prison system and is updated through reevaluation procedures periodically until his or her release.

The Prison Environment

Doing time in prison is difficult, particularly for the first-time offender. Inmates enter an environment that has a distinct set of behavioral norms, but "virtually everyone on their way to prison lacks accurate information about what to expect" (Zoukis, 2017, p. 2). Mentor inmates willing to explain the various expectations can help new inmates learn prison etiquette. This etiquette encompasses every social aspect of the prison, ranging from providing privacy to fellow inmates while they are taking a shower or using the restroom, seating arrangements while dining or watching television, and to what extent social interactions between races is considered acceptable at that particular facility. Much of this etiquette depends on each prison's demographics, security level, and administrative culture.

Much has been written regarding offender and inmate values, including the prison subculture. Early scholars debated whether a distinct prison culture existed and, if it did, the causes of such a subculture. Inmate behavior could be a result of various "pains of imprisonment" such as deprivations of freedom, security, autonomy, goods and services, and lack of access to heterosexual relationships (Sykes, 1958). The pains of imprisonment can result in significant emotional distress and create a negative and sometimes dangerous prison climate (Leigey & Ryder, 2015; Rocheleau, 2013). Alternatively, prison behavior might be derived from a set of deviant behaviors that originate outside of prison and are simply concentrated within the institution (Irwin & Cressey, 1962). For example, more than half (54%) of state prisoners are incarcerated due to a conviction for a violent offense (Carson, 2018). Thus, it should be no surprise that violent behavior sometimes occurs within these prison settings or that prisons with a large proportion of violent offenders might have a higher violence rate than other facilities.

Benjamin Fleury-Steiner and Jamie Longazel (2014) revisited the pains of imprisonment identified by Sykes. They found that the original findings are still relevant, but changes in the correctional system in the era of penal harm made the deprivations worse. They developed an inventory of the pains of *mass* imprisonment: containment, exploitation, coercion, isolation, and brutality. Aggressive incapacitation replaced the goal of rehabilitation with containment. The deprivation of goods and services has been enhanced by exploiting inmates for financial profit through low-wage prison labor and by charging for housing and medical care. Women prisoners are subjected to sexual coercion by male guards. Mass imprisonment contributed to special housing units and thousands of prisoners held in solitary confinement. The loss of security is compounded by the brutality of prison guards.

It is also possible that the pains of imprisonment are experienced and dealt with differently among certain groups of inmates. For example, sex offenders and inmates who are serving life sentences often experience prison differently than other inmates (Leigey, 2015; Zoukis, 2017). Contemporary research has found evidence that both inmate and prison characteristics are responsible for the inmate subculture (Cihan,

Davidson, & Sorensen, 2017; Marcum, Hilinski-Rosick, & Freiburger, 2014; Steiner, Ellison, Butler, & Cain, 2017).

Once incarcerated in prison, the inmate has two basic choices: (a) become a part of the inmate subculture/society or (b) attempt to serve one's sentence isolated from the rest of the inmates. Doing time isolated from the inmate population is an option few offenders can tolerate psychologically and emotionally. The inmate value system has two primary goals: (1) getting out as soon as possible and (2) making life as tolerable as possible while in prison. Getting out could mean anything from parole to escape. Making life tolerable in prison may include affiliating with a particular inmate group, selling illegal goods and providing illegal services, and working with the prison administration in areas of mutual interest and benefit. However, too much interaction with the prison administration risks labeling an inmate as a snitch. This label could result in increased victimization or the inmate being sent to protective custody within the facility. Protective custody typically involves a significantly reduced quality of life as the inmate will likely be isolated in a cell with limited social opportunities or ability to move outside of his/her cell. Obviously, this reality creates a strong incentive to become part of the inmate subculture.

Critical to the quality of life in a given prison environment is the correctional administrative leadership. Prison administrators must set policies and regulate activities in two important correctional contexts: (a) security and (b) treatment. Although the current correctional focus seems to be on security and custody rather than treatment, rehabilitation and other treatment programs are indispensable to correctional administrators, both for changing criminal behavior and attitudes and for minimizing inmate adjustment problems in the prison environment (Duwe, 2017). Cognitive behavior therapy programs improve decision-making and problem-solving skills and target criminogenic risk factors such as antisocial cognition and chemical dependency. These programs have had the best outcomes in reducing disciplinary infractions. Social support interventions that reduce associations with antisocial peers and help offenders develop prosocial sources of support have also been effective in decreasing misconduct. Prison visitation is the most prominent source of prosocial support for prisoners. The effects of facility education programs on inmate misconduct are generally positive, particularly post-secondary programming.

Progressive correctional administrators work hard to minimize any conflicts between security officers and treatment professionals, which inmates may be able to intentionally or unintentionally exploit. If administrative leaders do not resolve personnel problems effectively, the result is poor morale as well as the potential for staff corruption. Where corruption in a prison environment has been allowed to evolve, correctional personnel have been involved in a variety of illegal and unethical actions ranging from absconding with prison property (e.g., food) to engaging in sexual misconduct with inmates.

Inmate Misconduct

As with the development of the prison subculture, prison misconduct is explained by both inmate characteristics and the prison's ability to control behavior (Randol & Campbell, 2017; Zoukis, 2017). Not surprisingly, most research finds that misconduct occurs more often in higher security facilities (Griffin & Hepburn, 2013). Lower security facilities hold inmates whose evaluations did not show them to be security risks, and inmates housed in these facilities have more to lose by breaking the rules. Administrative decisions can also impact social control within the facility. For example, the elimination of an extended visitation program designed for inmates with good behavior reduced the inmates' incentive to follow the rules (Leigey, 2015). Social control is also maintained by the inmates themselves through the prison subculture and organized gangs within the facility. These inmate organizations often set rules that impact the entire inmate population. Inmates interviewed in one study described an environment in which prison "shot callers" used informal tactics to control violence and to reduce the chance of riots. They valued profit and peace and created rules to avoid any potential of a lockdown and the subsequent disruption of the underground economy (Trammell, 2009). Even inmates who were not affiliated with a gang or prison group followed the rules established by the prison subculture.

Despite the correctional institution's legal responsibility to ensure the safety of each inmate, violence is a reality in these settings. Examples of prison violence include: prisoner-on-prisoner assaults, prisoner-on-staff assaults, staff-on-prisoner assaults, suicide and attempted suicide, sexual victimization, and riots. It is difficult to quantify all the violence that occurs within prisons due to lack of official statistics and the likelihood that prisoners might not report their victimizations to prison officials. Overcrowding, inadequate and unhealthy food service, insecure facilities, the presence of mentally ill inmates, extensive use of solitary confinement, insufficient staff training, and frayed relationships between staff and prisoners make prisons ripe for violence. In April 2018, rioting at Lee Correctional Institution, a maximum-security prison in South Carolina, lasted for 8 hours and resulted in the death of seven inmates and injuries to 17 others. The riot was one of the deadliest in recent history, and there were allegations that officers did little to curb the violence when the fighting broke out and did not render assistance as quickly as they could have (Wang & Berman, 2018). South Carolina imprisoned more than 20,400 inmates in 2017; the number of inmates killed in the state's prisons quadrupled from three in 2015 to 12 in 2017.

Data on prison violence is collected sporadically. The media generally report only sensational events such as riots. The most recent government report shows that assaults occur in approximately 85% of facilities in a given year, with most prisons reporting only one or two assaults per year (Bureau of Justice Statistics, 2005). However, survey results often show much higher rates of violent victimization (Wolff, Blitz, Shi, Siegel, & Bachman, 2007). A sample of more than 7,000 inmates reported 6-month inmate-on-inmate victimization rates of 21%—10 times higher than the victimization rate outside prison walls (Wolff, Shi, & Siegel, 2009). Most prison inmates have a history of being victimized as children and adults. The ecology of prison environments may produce conditions that encourage victimization.

Increasing attention has been directed toward understanding the prevalence and reasons for sexual assault and rape within prisons. In 2003, Congress passed the Prison Rape Elimination Act (PREA), which required a zero-tolerance stance regarding prison sexual victimization and provided monetary assistance to create 40 national standards that have assisted in the reduction of prison rape (Struckman-Johnson & Struckman-Johnson, 2013). Official statistics show that in a 12 month period, approximately 2% of inmates report being sexually victimized by another inmate, with another 2.4% reporting being victimized by a member of the prison staff (Beck, Berzofsky, Caspar, & Krebs, 2013). However, many scholars suspect that prison rape is vastly underreported. Victims might feel embarrassed, might be afraid of retaliation from the perpetrator, or might perceive that reporting the sexual offense would be viewed by the prison culture as equivalent to snitching (Garland & Wilson, 2012; Miller, 2010). Although no type of inmate is fully protected from sexual violence, victims are often recently incarcerated, smaller, and younger than their perpetrators (Morash, Jeong, Bohmert, & Bush, 2012).

All prisons use some form of solitary confinement to separate inmates who commit serious infractions from the general population (Kappeler & Potter, 2018). Whether called isolation, restricted housing, special housing units, disciplinary segregation, administrative segregation, or protective custody, all terms refer to confinement that exerts maximum control over the individual in an isolated cell for an average of 23 hours a day with limited human interaction or constructive activity. Another response to the increased violence in prisons was the supermax institution. These facilities and extensive use of solitary confinement were direct outgrowths of the punitive ideology of the penal harm movement.

Although exact definitions of *supermax* vary (Butler, Griffin, & Johnson, 2012), all prisoners in these institutions are confined in isolation in concrete cells that measure 7 × 12 feet; they are subject to extraordinary control and severe deprivation. Supermax prisons were designed to control "the worst of the worst." The isolating architecture of supermax institutions and the technology of control were designed to deprive, diminish, and punish. Correctional staff respond to prisoners through force and repression. The potential for abuse inheres in the structure of the prison. Advocates of supermax prisons argue that they are needed to house the most dangerous and disruptive offenders. Critics worry that the stringent conditions at supermax facilities make inmates angrier and more violent (Mears, 2013).

The Effects of Imprisonment

Since 2000, new demographic profiles have emerged for inmates. As states have attempted to curb the use of prisons for low-level drug and property offenses, they have also increased the sentence length for serious violent crimes (Courtney, Eppler-Epstein, Pelletier, King, & Lei, 2017). Thus, a larger proportion of prisoners are serving longer prison terms than ever before. The effects of imprisonment are varied. Prisons have often been referred to as academies or training centers for criminal behavior, since many offenders leave prison possessing more criminal skills than when they entered. For many prison administrators, the challenge changed from sending inmates back to the community better than when they entered to not sending them back worse than when they came in!

Inmates who have served extended periods of time in prison often become institutionalized. Because of the highly regimented nature of prison life, institutionalized offenders may experience a phobic reaction to life outside prison walls. Such regimentation, while perhaps often necessary, encourages obedience rather than discipline. That is, inmates follow orders rather than developing an internal value system through which the offender takes more responsibility for his or her actions. After years of being told when to eat, sleep, go to work, and visit with one's family, inmates find it difficult to make decisions for themselves when released into outside society. After being banished from society and living a monotonous, relentless existence, adjusting to completely different circumstances is difficult.

The hope of someday leaving prison is an important motivation for most offenders. However, many inmates receive life sentences without the possibility of parole; they will die in prison. These inmates generally avoid trouble and often become mentors for younger inmates. Long term imprisonment appears to encourage a number of coping mechanisms that help offenders organize their lives in as meaningful a way as possible. Coping methods include dedication to work assignments, becoming involved in creative expressions such as art, caring for other inmates, and developing a stronger adherence to religious principles (Johnson & Dobrzanska, 2005; Leigey, 2015).

Summary

The prison inmate's world is often confusing and ambiguous. The prison environment can be frustrating for the correctional staff as well as for the inmate population. Most offenders are classified informally by the public and correctional personnel; the label *convict* remains with the offender beyond the sentence he or she received. A new prison inmate is formally classified during the first few weeks of prison. The classification addresses security concerns, physical and mental health profiles, educational background, vocational skills, religious affiliations, and type of offense(s) committed. The classification determines the security level as well as recommended treatment programs.

The prison environment is difficult for inmates, particularly first-time offenders. The prison culture is unique among all subcultures. In order for inmates to live and cope within the walls, they must make one of two basic choices: (a) become a part of the inmate subculture, or (b) attempt to serve their sentence isolated from the rest of the other inmates. An inmate with a lengthy sentence may find isolation an intolerable experience. Therefore, most inmates find it necessary to adjust and gain membership within the inmate society. The inmate value system has two primary goals: (1) getting out of prison as soon as possible, and (2) making life as tolerable as possible while in prison. Inmates learn quickly how to act with other inmates and how to act with correctional staff. An inmate's relationship with other inmates and the correctional staff is usually based on these two primary goals.

Correctional staff must provide a safe environment for inmates and staff alike while also providing treatment and programs to help inmates live a productive life outside of prison. This task is complicated by the unique setting, the volatility of the population group housed inside the facility, and the possibility that taking steps to punish those who engage in misconduct (e.g., isolation) might make things worse rather than better. Prison life is affected by the quality and training of the professional staff, the security level of a particular institution, and the traits of those inmates who are housed in the prison.

Bust or Parole?

Your name is Nancy. You are 45 years old and have served 12 years of a 20-year sentence for armed robbery. This is the second time around for you.

The last time you were in the "joint" was for burglary; you did 3 years on that sentence and made parole. You stayed straight for almost 2 years before you got into trouble again. Several of your friends finally convinced you to go along as the lookout on an easy bank score. Unfortunately, it did not turn out to be so easy. The bank's security officers opened fire on your two friends as they left the bank, killing one of them and wounding the other. You quickly surrendered without a struggle. You knew armed robbery was not for you, and you have always regretted being involved in that crime.

The 12 years you have served on your present sentence have not been easy ones. The inmates in your prison are a new breed, generally younger and more aggressive. Violence on the inside has increased; there are more suicides and assaults than ever before. Although the years have been hard, you have tried to make the most of them. You have earned your high school diploma and have even taken several additional college-level courses in accounting. In response to the public's demand to "get tough" on crime, many education and recreation programs have been severely cut back or discontinued altogether. This has made the general environment inside worse than ever.

Your brother, who owns a small business, has offered to employ you if you make parole. With your good behavior, your personal efforts toward rehabilitation, and your brother's offer, your chances of making parole are excellent. You realize that you have to stay straight this time or resign yourself to spending most of your remaining years in prison. You really want to make it this time, but there is some trouble brewing in your cell house that could blow your chances for parole sky high and even pose a threat to your own life.

A great deal of illegal drug activity is going on in your cell block. Although drug traffic in most prisons is rather common, in your institution the correctional officers are heavily involved in the illicit drug sales and distribution. An increasing number of women are also submitting to sex with several of the male officers as a means of paying for the drugs and, in some cases, earning extra money. In fact, rumor has it that the chief of security is behind most of it, and that many of the lieutenants and captains turn their heads.

Last night, you witnessed an inmate being badly beaten by a correctional officer because she had failed to pay for her drugs and would not agree to have sex with the officer to compensate for her debt. Today, the prison administration has placed the facility on lockdown and is conducting an investigation into the assault. However, the word is also out that the correctional officer has framed another inmate as the attacker. Both the correctional officers and inmates are eager to get the investigation complete and the lockdown lifted so the drug-related prison economy can continue. The easiest thing for you to do would be to keep quiet and let the innocent inmate be punished for the attack. However, you worry that this inmate will not be able to cope with the punishment of an extended stay in segregation.

You have considered going to the prison superintendent, Dr. Williams, whom you are certain is not involved in the drug traffic. You know him to be an experienced and progressive corrections administrator. However, you are concerned that if you tell the superintendent the truth, the inmates and correctional officers will label you as a snitch. This could potentially result in you being set up for an attack or being falsely accused of misconduct. Even if the administrator believes you and wants to protect you from retaliation, this protection would likely come in the form of segregation. Yu can sit tight or go to Dr. Williams and tell him what is going on. You wonder whether or not you can really trust the superintendent. If you do tell him what is going on, will he believe you? Will he return you to the cell block to be at the mercy of those inmates and correctional officers you reported? A trip to Dr. Williams might help your chances for parole or, on the other hand, might endanger your personal safety.

Questions for Discussion

Nancy is in a dilemma not primarily of her making. Are there outside persons Nancy could go to? Who is responsible for identifying the perpetrator of the attack? How do you think this kind of corrupt situation develops in prison, and what can be done to provide safeguards against such corrupt practices?

Case 2

Six Months to Go

A year ago the biggest concern in your life was finishing college. Now your biggest concern is your own personal safety. Never in a million years did you dream that you would be spending year 20 of your life in a state prison. As a sociology major in college, you studied about crime, criminals, and prisons but learned nothing that prepared you for your situation now. The constant noise of steel and concrete; the smell of bodies, cigarettes, and old buildings; the inability to go where you want to go, eat what you want to eat—all this is foreign and overwhelming.

Sure, you smoked some grass and sometimes used pills to stay up and study for exams when you were in college; a lot of other students did the same. You never expected to get "busted" for selling a small amount of marijuana and uppers to an acquaintance who turned out to be a narcotics officer. But you did. Since it was your first offense, your lawyer said probation was a sure thing. Unfortunately for you, you got a judge who was fed up with drug abuse. He decided that it was time to crack down, and he used you as an example, sentencing you to 3 years in the state prison. When he pronounced sentence, the world came crashing down on you and your family.

Your experiences in prison have left you despondent. During those first few months of incarceration, you felt hopeless. Your family, although upset and embarrassed, has stuck by you, and their visits momentarily boost your spirits. The efforts of a young prison counselor and the support of your family have kept you going. Only 6 months remain on your sentence before you come up for parole. You have "kept your nose clean" with the prison staff and other inmates.

Last night a terrible incident occurred. Your 18-year-old cell mate, Mario, was brutally raped and beaten by four older inmates, who threatened that you would suffer the same fate if you reported them. You remember only too well the whistles and taunts directed toward you during the first several days you were in the cell block. You realize

70

that your size and athletic conditioning protected you. Your cell mate, being smaller and weaker, had no such natural defense qualities. You also realize that if you report them, the four inmates are likely to carry out their threat. Still, you cannot rid yourself of the rage and sickness you feel over your friend's torment and humiliation. You know that he might be attacked again. Yet, you are also concerned about your own survival and well-being.

You have continued to be an avid reader while incarcerated. While in the prison law library doing some research for a fellow inmate, you learned about a federal law called the Prison Rape Elimination Act. The only employee you trust in the prison is the young counselor. Not having been at the prison very long, he has only limited influence with the prison administration. Nevertheless, he is enthusiastic and well intentioned. You wonder if the counselor can use the law to convince prison administrators to take action—and if there will be any protection for you if you report the perpetrators.

Questions for Discussion

What does the Prison Rape Elimination Act require of prison officials in protecting inmates from the threat of sexual assault? Did the administration do enough to protect Mario from such abuse? What programs or other opportunities could have been provided for most of the prison's inmates that might have helped alleviate the problem of sexual assault?

Case 3

An Expression of Grief

You are known as Willy throughout the prison. You are serving 15 years on a manslaughter conviction. Before your present conviction, you were sentenced to probation on an assault and battery charge. Now a model inmate, you stick pretty much to yourself and give no one any trouble. Since being in prison you have become interested in religion and spend a great deal of your time reading and studying the Bible.

You recently began receiving weekly letters from your younger sister about your father, who was hospitalized again for a terminal liver ailment. Rereading the letters brought back many memories of your childhood. Your father worked long and hard in the coal mines of Kentucky to support his wife and seven children. You have a tremendous amount of respect for your father and contrast your failures with his dedication. You decided to request a special pass from the warden to visit your sick and dying father. The warden considered your request but decided to reject it because of your maximum security classification. You were upset and frustrated.

Several days later the sky fell in. You received a call from your sister telling you that your father had died and that the funeral would be in two days. You again approached the warden for permission to attend your father's funeral. The warden sympathized with your plight but again declined your request, for the same reasons given previously. You flew into a rage; the guards had to subdue you while the prison physician gave you a sedative. The assistant warden in charge of treatment then had a guard escort you to the chapel for personal counseling with the institutional chaplain.

You are now waiting for the chaplain. Other inmates have told you that security is weak in this area of the prison. Should you sneak out the back entrance of the chapel and hide in the milk truck that is parked there each morning? Every inmate in the institution knows about this escape route, and you now have the opportunity to take advantage of it. What should you do? Sure, they would pick you up in a couple of days, but not before you got home for your father's funeral. Of course, you wouldn't make trustee in 6 months as the warden has promised. Your positive prison record wouldn't be so positive anymore. But what is more important, your father's funeral or your prison record? Your grief over your father's death and your anger over two denials of a pass to leave the prison swirl through your mind as you try to decide what to do.

Questions for Discussion

What could the administration have done differently to ease the crisis situation with Willy? Could they have let him talk with his father on the telephone? Should he have been left alone in the chapel? Should they have provided counseling services for him at an earlier date?

Something for Nothing?

Your name is Ronnie Denver, and you are 18 years old. Your mother, a registered nurse, divorced your father years ago. Although she had several relationships with other men in the years following the divorce, none ever worked out on a permanent basis. She also had several bouts with alcohol and amphetamine abuse. You have not seen your father since the divorce.

Everyone has always remarked how easygoing you are, how well you roll with the punches. Sure, you have gotten in trouble several times. As a juvenile, you and two friends were caught stealing a car for a joyride. Twice you were apprehended for possession of amphetamines. The judge described your third possession charge as the last straw, and he sentenced you to 9 months in the city jail. You smiled politely as you received your sentence, thinking that the city jail could not be any worse than the boring high school you have been attending.

When you arrived for processing at the jail you were surprised at the whistles and catcalls of the other inmates as you walked with the guard through the recreation yard to your cell block. You just smiled back and gave the peace symbol in hopes of letting the other prisoners know that you wanted to get along with them. The next morning the control-station guard sounded the bell and opened the gates. The inmates poured out of their cells, heading for the chow hall. Since you were not hungry, you decided to stay in your cell and read a western you had borrowed from one of your cell mates.

You look up from your book to find a big burly inmate standing in your doorway. "Hi kid," he says with a cold stare.

"Hello. My name is Ronnie Denver," you respond, eager to make your first friend.

"I know," the visitor replies. "My name is Al. Most guys in here call me 'Big Al.'" He goes on to explain that things are different in jails and prisons—in ways that people on the outside cannot understand. He

74

stresses that in order to have a "safe stay," it is best to have good friends who will stand up for you.

Although you do not completely understand what Big Al is trying to say, you are relieved at having made a friend so quickly. Al notices the book in your hand and inquires if you like to read. You indicate that you do and that you hope to read your way through your sentence if you can get enough books. Big Al assures you that you will not have any problem getting books, since he is personal friends with the jail's librarian. As he describes the kinds of books he likes to read, Al reaches into his shirt pocket and pulls out a pack of cigarettes. Lighting one, he asks you if you smoke. "Only menthol," you reply. Al assures you that he can supply you with plenty of menthol cigarettes, since the guy who works in the inmate canteen owes him a number of favors.

As Al turns to leave, he says, "It gets very lonely in here, Ronnie, and we have to take care of each other. Just remember, Big Al takes care of his own. You just be my friend." Needless to say, you are a little overwhelmed by his concern and generosity concerning some of the things he said to you. Should you respond to his friendship? What will he want in return? He does seem to know the ropes. What will happen if you decide to remain somewhat aloof and do your time by yourself?

Questions for Discussion

Is doing time primarily a matter of survival in which an inmate must learn how to "get along?" Are there limits to what you, as Ronnie, should be willing to do? If so, how do you impose those limits? What roles do correctional officers and counselors play in protecting vulnerable inmates like Ronnie? What are their responsibilities?

Case 5

What's for Supper?

Your name is Harriet, but most of the other inmates at the state women's prison call you Sis. You earned the affectionate nickname by being a "big sister" to most of the women in the prison, especially the younger ones. You come up for parole in 2 months, and you have been told that your chances are good. You have completed 3 years of a 5-year sentence for voluntary manslaughter. One of the many drunken squabbles between you and your husband had ended with you holding a gun in your hand and him lying dead on the floor. Although the nightmares still come from time to time, you can live with what happened now. It is behind you. Besides, you have a 9-year-old daughter who is living with your mother and waiting patiently for your return. Helping the other girls at the prison has been therapeutic for you. You are proud of their confidence in you and your established reputation of being firm but offering an understanding ear.

The food at your institution has never been good, but it is becoming unbearable. The meals consist mostly of starches; meat is served infrequently and is always of inferior quality. The poor selection of food is bad enough, but the preparation is even worse. Since you are a respected leader of the other inmates, it had fallen to you to go to the prison superintendent and complain. Rather than offering assurances that she would look into the complaints, she told you to file a grievance and snapped that since she had not received any grievances in writing, you must simply be trying to stir up trouble. As she turned to walk away, the superintendent asked if you didn't have a parole coming up soon.

Tensions continued to mount. For many, mealtimes were the high points of the day. The repeated disappointment of receiving stale bread, gristle, and not enough coffee created a potentially explosive situation. Each mealtime in the dining room was becoming more tense. There had already been several minor confrontations between the inmates and the guards.

Now a group of girls want you to endorse a dining-hall protest over the poor food. Because of the high level of emotions, you realize that the protest could easily escalate into a full-blown disturbance. You are sitting on a powder keg that could explode during any meal. You know there is reason to protest, but you also realize that if a serious distur- bance occurs, you and the others might lose more than you can ever hope to gain, including your parole. On the other hand, the superinten- dent and her administration have failed to make any significant improvements regarding the food quality.

If you do not support the protest, you might lose the respect of the girls. Should you approach the superintendent again? Should you just sit tight and see what happens? Should you go ahead and endorse the protest, hoping that it remains peaceful? There is no easy way to go, and time is running out.

Questions for Discussion

Many riots have started in prison mess halls. Could the superinten- dent have done more to address the complaints about the food? Should Sis have relied so much on the inmate grievance system? Is it too late to avert the prospect of a mess-hall confrontation?

Case 6

Home Sweet Home

Next Wednesday you will be walking out the front gates of the prison as a free man. You just served 10 years on your third hitch. You have spent 30 of the last 40 years of your life behind bars. Your disposition has softened after 62 years of life's ups and downs. You have no excuses left; you feel that the time you got was coming to you. In fact, the last hitch was one you purposely set up.

When you were released the last time, it was a cold gray morning in February. There was no one waiting for you; all your friends were in prison. You had been divorced for over 15 years, and your former wife had remarried. Your parents were dead, and your two sisters had given up on you long ago. There was no one to care about you like they did inside the joint. The sudden freedom was frightening—there were too many decisions to make in the free world.

You got a job as a busboy in a restaurant, but the hustle and bustle was too much. You were lonely; no one wanted to make friends with an old ex-con. Finally you couldn't copy any longer, so you stole all the money from the cash register during a lull in the business. You did not spend any of it. Instead you went home, had a beer, and waited. Once the restaurant manager realized you and the money were missing, he called the police. In less than two hours, the police arrived at your apartment and arrested you. You refused an attorney and told the judge that you would keep committing crimes until he sent you back. He reluctantly sentenced you to 10 years. You passed up parole each time it came around.

So here you are again. You have been measured for your new suit of street clothes, and your $150 check for transitional expenses has been processed. The labor department representative has arranged for you to have a stock-clerk job in a small grocery store in a nearby town. Your social worker has also arranged for you to stay in a small apartment near where you will work. You remember your last prerelease counseling session with her and how she offered all the words of encouragement a young, energetic, and well-meaning counselor could muster. You just smiled and nodded your approval. What good would it have done to burst her idealistic bubble? She could never understand how frightening the outside world was for you. All of her friends lived in the free world; none of yours did.

You know you ought to feel happy about leaving prison, but the truth is, you are miserable about it. You would like to be able to make it on the outside, but deep down inside you feel you are doomed before you start. The odds are against you, and you can already feel the loneliness eating away at you.

Questions for Discussion

What prerelease programs are available in the prison that would assist this inmate in preparing for release to the outside world? Are there any life-skills programs available through the prison education and/or treatment services departments? Is there a community-based intensive supervision program (ISP) that he can be referred to by his parole officer once he returns home? Would a halfway house placement be a suitable initial placement for him upon release from prison?

Case 7

The Prison Schoolhouse

You have been the director of education programs at Anyville State Prison for quite a number of years. The basic education and vocational classes follow a standard public-school schedule. Recruiting qualified teachers is not easy given the environment in which they will work. Most teachers have to drive quite a distance to the prison. Upon arrival, they must leave their phones and other belongings in their car, go through metal detectors, and stay confined to their classroom most of the day. The student population adds other complications. Inmates often lack the basic literacy and math skills needed to succeed. Many dropped out of school prior to high school and never learned the value of education. The biggest motivation for most of the students in prison is the automatic 30 days taken off sentences if an inmate earns a GED while in prison. Teachers endure a lot of stress and could easily find other jobs if not for their dedication to helping inmates better their lives.

Each year you send the annual school calendar to the superintendent. There has never been a problem in the past, but this year is different. A new superintendent recently took over; he has a reputation of being very autocratic and demanding. One morning he calls you to his office and tells you to change the schedule. He is irate that the school will be closed from the 18th of December until January 3 for the holidays. He pointedly makes it clear that the prison is not a public school—that it operates "24/7." He can't afford to have inmates sitting around doing nothing for three weeks. When you try to explain that the inmates and staff both need the break, he refuses to budge. You point out that it is difficult to recruit and retain good teachers, and that something like this could cause some of them to leave. He tells you they can all quit if they don't like it. As you get up to leave his office, the superintendent tells you ominously that he had better see inmates and teachers in school throughout the holidays.

Questions for Discussion

In addition to a less-than-understanding management style, it is obvious that the superintendent does not grasp the necessity of a break in the education routine during the holidays. What should (or can) you do?

Case 8

From Troublemaker to Peacemaker

As deputy warden of State Prison, it is your responsibility to make a recommendation to the warden regarding Raymond Angelo's request to be allowed to return to the general-population section of death row. Angelo's correctional history is quite a story. For the last 7 years, he has been for the most part isolated in administrative segregation on death row. He was originally sentenced to 10 years for drug dealing and armed robbery, but that was before he was implicated in the killing of a correctional officer.

For the first 3 years of his prison sentence, Raymond Angelo was a rabble–rouser, troublemaker, and on the wrong side of just about every correctional officer with whom he came in contact. Then Officer Edward Klein was stabbed to death. The inmate who stabbed him told investigators that Angelo provided the shank used to kill Officer Klein. The inmate who stabbed the correctional officer was sentenced to life without parole; Raymond Angelo was sentenced to death. Sometimes, you think to yourself, justice moves in strange and unpredictable ways.

Angelo raised so much hell during his first 6 months on death row that he was placed in the administrative segregation unit. That was before he got religion. Over the next 2 years, Angelo changed—meditating, praying, and reading religious literature instead of shouting and demanding. Then Angelo wrote a best-selling book on spiritual transformation and donated all the profits to a fund set up for Officer Klein's family. To top things off, it looks like his appeals may just carry some weight with the current court.

It seems simple enough—6 years of good behavior should get Angelo transferred back into death row's general population, where he could have more privileges. The problem is that correctional officers have long memories when one of their own is killed, and rightly so.

While some of the officers who have worked around Angelo are all right with his transfer, most of the other officers are against any change of status for him.

Questions for Discussion

What are some reasons correctional officers tend to develop negative attitudes about inmates who seem to change for the better? What about inmate perceptions regarding returning Angelo to death row's population? What are some possible positive and negative consequences for such a transfer? No question about it—you depend more on your correctional officers than on inmates, and you can't deny you have a warden's natural sense of suspicion about Angelo. Still, you want to do the right thing, and it isn't like you would be giving Angelo a walk. What will your decision be?

SECTION IV

The Correctional Officer

The correctional officer is an important key to the success of any correctional program. Correctional officers are responsible for institutional and program security, but they also have the potential to be change agents regarding the behavior and attitudes of the inmates they supervise.

In the introduction, we briefly cover some of the demands placed on the typical correctional officer. We then present eight cases to elicit your reaction to situations that include crisis intervention skills, peer-group pressures, and riot control.

Introduction

The potential impact of correctional personnel, particularly security officers, on the rehabilitation and resocialization of offenders is too frequently given only brief recognition by authorities in the correctional treatment process. In correctional institutions, correctional security personnel have the most contact and interaction with offenders (Dial, 2010). Many former prisoners do not remember the names of prison counselors or caseworker, but they recall vividly the names and personalities of many of the correctional officers. The influence of correctional officers on correctional goals is an important topic that is infrequently explored.

Employment

Over two-thirds of the employees in corrections are correctional officers, who numbered 428,870 in 2017 (Bureau of Labor Statistics,

2018). In terms of sheer numbers, security personnel are an extremely important component of the correctional workforce. Their behavior affects the general environment of custodial facilities and the mood of the inmate population. Traditionally, the job of a correctional officer was one of the least prestigious jobs in the justice system, requiring no formal education and offering minimal training. Today, federal correctional officers must have a bachelor's degree and experience (Stohr & Walsh, 2018). Most jails and prisons do not require postsecondary education. The training for new hires in correctional work does not approach the level for police departments.

Typically, a high school diploma is required (with incentive pay for an undergraduate degree) along with successful completion of a civil service examination. Training for correctional officers varies widely among the states. Frequently, however, training for new officers consists of a few weeks of classroom instruction. The average salary for correctional officers in 2017 was $47,600 (Bureau of Labor Statistics, 2018). Salary differs by locality, and the entry-level salary is often in the $25,000 range. Given the dangers and stress inherent in the job (Steiner & Wooldredge, 2017), this salary is often not enough to attract highly qualified applicants. In most prisons, the bulk of the population is poor and economically disadvantaged. In this respect, the prisoners are probably similar to their keepers, since correctional officers are also employed primarily from economically disadvantaged regions.

Correctional Officer and Inmate Attitudes

Historically, correctional officers, like their police counterparts, have been organized along paramilitary lines and were expected to employ rigorous rule enforcement and coercion to maintain institutional security. Supervisory officers usually judge their subordinate officers' work performance on the basis of how "quietly" their work assignments are completed, including the absence of any problems regarding an officer's performance.

Correctional officers often complain about having unclear rules or receiving conflicting orders from more than one person (Steiner & Wooldredge, 2015). The uncertainty and contradictory expectations can lead correctional officers to believe that they are on their own in carrying out assignments and dealing with inmates. Some correctional officers are authoritative when dealing with inmates but also provide human services; others are custodial and authoritarian—more likely to enforce their authority than the rules (Johnson, Rocheleau, & Alison, 2017).

Correctional officers are significantly outnumbered by inmates and are confined in close quarters with them. Officers learn quickly that, in many respects, they are just as much captive as the inmates. It should not be surprising, therefore, that subcultures develop among correctional officers just as they do with inmates. Occupational attitudes common within this subculture include: always go to the aide of an officer in danger; keep your cool; back fellow officers' decisions; carry your own weight; and defer to the experience of veteran officers. Further, correctional officers are expected not to admit to mistakes, trust inmates, get too close to inmates, or be lenient with inmates (Whitehead, Dodson, & Edwards, 2013). Succumbing to any of these temptations is viewed as a sign of weakness. The subculture combined with correctional policies and training that limit the interaction of staff with prisoners contribute to a lack of communication. Without communication, there is little opportunity to find common ground with inmates or to expose stereotypes as inaccurate.

The media portray serious offenders as dangerous and unpredictable. These depictions affect officer attitudes and make them fearful for their safety. Particularly in maximum-security prisons, correctional officers view prisoners as "dangerous others" (Johnson et al., 2017). Such attitudes result in a prison subculture that emphasizes punishment, control, and deprivation. Correctional officers feel the tension generated by the possibility of major assaults or riots within the prison population (Gordon & Baker, 2017; Martin, Lichtenstein, Jenkot, & Forde, 2012). Despite these barriers, correctional officers recognize that they must gain and maintain the cooperation of inmates. For that to occur, offenders expect correctional officers to be reasonable and consistent and to refrain from engaging in overly strict rule enforcement. Discretionary decision making takes place in the enforcement of rules (Johnson et al., 2017). Some officers underenforce the rules to keep the prison running smoothly and to reduce tension. They adopt a negotiation model that enforces rules fairly but also keeps operations running smoothly Service-oriented officers can provide goods and services, act as advocates or referral agents, and help with institutional adjustment problems.

State penal systems vary as to the emphasis on rehabilitation and treatment; the attitudes of officers may be influenced by the goals of the system. Researchers surveyed correctional officers in California and Minnesota (Lerman & Page, 2012). While officers from both states expressed support for specific rehabilitative programs, officers from Minnesota were significantly more likely than those from California to favor rehabilitation as a proper goal for the prison system—an outcome of officers adapting to their state's policies.

Prison administrators may be fighting an uphill battle to convince some correctional officers to embrace the treatment goal. For instance, one state mandated that all new hires into the prison system be given a training session reinforcing how positive behavior and treatment programs were a priority within the department. Following the 2-hour training session, correctional officers were found to be less receptive to the treatment and rehabilitation programs compared to the maintenance, clerical, and treatment staff (Young, Antonio, & Wingeard, 2009). The correctional officer subculture will likely reinforce and strengthen these preexisting attitudes.

Treatment-oriented personnel often express concern about the conflict between custodial care and treatment needs; the relationship has historically been one of opposition. What treatment personnel may attempt to do, security personnel can sometimes destroy and vice-versa. Disciplinary infractions and other custodial considerations can prevent, hamper, or terminate inmate involvement in the institution's treatment programs (e.g., academic, counseling, vocational, etc.). While institutional rules and regulations play a vital role in the correctional process, unnecessary rules and the regimens of daily prison life often impede the development of individual inmate responsibility and the ability to accept treatment. Administrators must insure that the institution's goals are not harmed by conflict between treatment staff and correctional officers.

Prison Work

Administrators must strive to create a workplace that reduces the stress of correctional work. High levels of stress lead to employee turnover and lower levels of job satisfaction and commitment (Lambert, Worley & Worley, 2018). Two major concerns of correctional officers are personal safety and the strain of receiving conflicting orders and guidance. Officers who self-reported following the rules had higher levels of work stress. The prison environment can be particularly difficult for female and younger officers (Cheeseman & Downey, 2012; Dial, Downey, & Goodlin, 2010). The job has also been found to increase tension in officers' family life outside the prison, which can then lead to increased stress and lower job satisfaction (Armstrong, Atkin-Plunk, & Wells, 2015).

Officers who are stressed and dissatisfied with their jobs can eventually become burned out (Griffin, Hogan, Lambert, Gail, & Baker, 2010). Burnout among correctional officers can have significant consequences on the prison operation (Gould, Watson, Price, & Valliant, 2012). For example, correctional officers suffering from burnout often fail to show up to work on a regular basis, have more negative perceptions toward correctional treatment, and may ultimately be less committed to the job (Lambert, Barton-Bellessa, & Hogan, 2015). Obviously, these outcomes can undermine the efficiency and effectiveness of the prison's goals.

Perceptions of inmates by correctional officers affect stress levels. If an officer perceives inmates as easy to manage, that officer is more likely to use verbal intervention strategies for control rather than physical restraint or the use of formal disciplinary procedures (Lambert et al., 2018). Inmates, in turn, are more likely to respect that officer and to be cooperative. If an officer perceives that the only way to manage inmates is to exert force or to invoke disciplinary procedures, he or she is more likely to be tense and anxious.

Supervisory support is a critical workplace resource. In one study, officer job stress and satisfaction were significantly related to supervisor support (Hartley, Davida, Marquart, & Mullings, 2013). Officers appreciated supervisors who "stand by us and not the offender" (p. 334). Supervisors need to provide support, equipment, and training so officers feel less at risk (Lambert et al., 2018). Administrators need to select and train supervisors carefully because supervisors play a vital role in developing professionalism. They should have the knowledge and experience to help officers address problems effectively. Supervisors also need to shield officers from negative peer pressure to bend or break the rules—that is, to engage in staff misconduct.

Research has indicated that staff misconduct is common within correctional facilities (Ross, Tewksbury, & Rolfe, 2016). Deviance by officers has a debilitating effect on the institution, affecting other correctional officers, corrections workers, administrators, and inmates. Misconduct against inmates might include actions such as abuse of authority, failure to provide medical care, theft of inmate property, discrimination toward certain inmates, excessive force, or sexual assaults (Rembert & Henderson, 2014; Ross, 2013). Corruption includes accepting bribes or sexual favors from inmates to smuggle cell phones, drugs, and other goods (CAPI, 2016). Administrators have been implicated in kickbacks from private suppliers and for covering up violations by officers.

Researchers found that staff members with poor pay and those who reported conflicting instructions from supervisors were more likely to engage in certain types of misconduct (Worley & Worley, 2016). While not an excuse for misconduct, it is possible to see how underpaid correctional officers who are under a great deal of stress and are not given clear directions from their superiors can be tempted to cross the professional boundaries expected of them. Policy makers and correctional administrators must address these issues to create a setting that serves institutional goals, maintains high morale among the correctional officers who interact with the offenders on a daily basis, and to eliminate prison staff misconduct.

Summary

Over two-thirds of correctional institutional employees are correctional officers. This ratio is the result of traditional views concerning roles, correctional philosophies, and building designs. Both the expectations of society and legal requirements make the custodial role the main function of the correctional system. Correctional officers are normal people placed in abnormal conditions. When great numbers are to be managed by a limited staff, there must be some means of control. This control has typically taken the form of a paramilitary custody model, which is not particularly suited for helping or treatment methods. While it is necessary to maintain control of inmates, there are varying perspectives on how and why tasks should be performed. Some institutions emphasize treatment within the parameters of a secure environment.

Although correctional officers have more contact with inmates, their roles in treatment are often underutilized. Training regarding perspectives on inmates and uniformity of instructions regarding the role of correctional officers can create a less stressful work environment and facilitate cooperation. Supervisory support is essential in helping officers do their work effectively.

Case 1

The First Day

You are a 25-year-old correctional officer, and this is your first day on the job. You have recently completed eight weeks of training at the Department of Corrections training academy, where you developed some degree of expertise in such areas as behavior control, self-defense, and general security administration. You have also completed 2 years of college, earning an Associate of Science degree in Criminal Justice, and you plan to continue studying and to earn a bachelor's degree in the same field.

You have been assigned as an officer on the midnight to 7:00 AM shift in the state prison, a maximum-security institution housing about 2,000 inmates. The facility was originally built in the early 1930s to house no more than 1,200 inmates. Aside from obvious problems created by confining too many inmates in too little space, other factors such as poor lighting and ventilation, long narrow corridors, and fortress-like construction have created a rather depressing and negative atmosphere. Because of your education and academy training, you are confident of your ability to perform your assigned duties in a highly professional manner. You feel that you will be able to communicate well with inmates and prison staff alike. In fact, at the academy you were described as one of the "new breed" of correctional officers—better educated, more understanding, and highly competent.

After reporting to work, you went directly to roll call. The shift supervisor informed you that daily work assignments are distributed on the basis of seniority; you were assigned to duty on a cell block in the special management unit (SMU). The other corrections officers smiled and laughed for no apparent reason. Although you had expected a warmer reception at roll call, you tried to shake it off and accepted the unexpected behavior as a challenge to prove yourself worthy of the friendship and respect of the other officers.

The supervisor didn't tell you where the SMU was located, so you asked another officer for directions. He pointed you in the general direction and left you with the impression that he was glad it was you going there rather than him. Your confidence began to deteriorate. You became nervous about being new on the job and even more uncomfortable because no one seemed to care. The academy instructors taught you how to get along with your fellow officers and to display a restrained friendliness toward the inmates, but applying that training was proving to be very difficult.

At the end of your first 8-hour tour, you were disappointed, bewildered, and frustrated. You had tried to start a friendly conversation with the other officer on duty; his only response was, "Don't make no unnecessary enemies." Attempts to introduce yourself and converse with the inmates were even more disappointing. If they spoke at all, it was to describe you in insulting terms. Your first day of work ended with you having second thoughts about your job and what you were supposed to be doing—and with your self-worth in general.

Questions for Discussion

It seems apparent that the prison administration in this case is not particularly concerned with helping new officers adjust to the job. If they were concerned, what are some ways they could make new correctional officers' adjustment easier and more meaningful? Would a mentorship program, where new officers are assigned for a period of time to older and more experienced officers, be helpful? Even though the administration seems unconcerned, is there anything that you as the new officer can do to adjust to your job more effectively?

Case 2

A Legacy of Corruption

You are a young woman, born and reared in a rural area in the South. Your father, a farmer, worked hard and saved his money. He provided you, your brother, two sisters, and your mother with a life of dignity and a sense of belonging—belonging to family, to town, and to country.

There was dignity, but no extras. Work was hard and income uncertain. Thriftiness was no mere virtue; it was a necessity. Your parents imbued you with the "American dream"—that hard work and education would make your life easier and more productive than theirs had been. By education, your parents meant high school and possibly some vocational training.

After high school, you and one of your best friends decided to join the Air Force, enlisting for the full 4 years. You were assigned to a base in the North, where you were able to learn a profession. Since your Air Force job was in personnel, you planned to seek work in a similar field when you were discharged.

When you returned to Midville and your family, you were ready to seek a career and a life of your own. Midville was home to you and you wanted to settle there, but there were no personnel jobs available. You felt that you would like to do something meaningful with your life. You wanted a job that would give you both security and a sense of accomplishment. You even considered reenlistment. Then you saw an advertisement:

> Correctional Officers needed at State Prison. Civil service position, fringe benefits, career opportunity. High school diploma required. Beginning salary $28,000. Apply at personnel office, main prison.

You couldn't believe your eyes! Twenty-eight thousand dollars a year! Who could live on that? After several more weeks in a fruitless job search, you decided to apply for a position. You could live at home for a while, and at least the work would be meaningful.

Six weeks later you completed your basic correctional officers' training. With your fellow trainees, you took and signed your oath of office.

> I do solemnly swear or affirm that I will faithfully and diligently perform all the duties required of me as an officer of the Department of Corrections and will observe and execute the laws, rules, and regulations passed and prescribed for the government thereof so far as the same concerns or pertains to my employment; that I will not ill treat or abuse any convict under my care, nor act contrary to the law, rules and regulations prescribed by legal authority, so help me God.

During the 3 years you have worked at the state prison, you have observed worsening conditions. You have been promoted twice, but your annual gross pay is still only $31,000. The inmate population has increased 40%, while there has only been a 10% increase in correctional officer positions. To make matters worse, the political and public mood has become increasingly negative. The positions for education and recreation specialists have been eliminated and 3 of the 8 counselor positions have been frozen. No education programs, little if any organized recreation, more inmates, fewer correctional officers, and restricted powers have resulted in dismal working conditions.

Increasing your frustration, you have learned that your captain and several other of your fellow officers are taking bribes from inmates in exchange for preferential assignments. You also heard reports that several of the female officers are earning extra income by having sex with some of the better connected inmates. Since you yourself have been propositioned twice during the last month, you have little doubt that the rumors are true. The last officer to complain about this particular captain was summarily dismissed and threatened with prosecution for possession of contraband (which he denied). The captain's father is a former warden of this prison, and his brother is the current business manager.

The situation has created a major crisis in your life. Your decision will be crucial because of its lasting implications for you. You value your personal integrity, and you believe in the intrinsic value of your profession—but you don't want to lose your job. You live in a beautiful, if depressed, economic area where few decent jobs exist. What should you do?

Questions for Discussion

Should you contact someone in the state office rather than the prison superintendent, or should you initially report your information to the prison internal affairs investigator? What might be the advantages or disadvantages of such a choice? How could the problem you are facing be resolved? How does public and political sentiment directly or indirectly affect the working conditions?

Case 3

Man in the Middle

The memo from the warden is unmistakably clear:

> All fighting, assaults, confrontations, loud arguments, and other contentious interactions between inmates are to be reported in writing at the end of each shift. Participants are to be placed in administrative segregation for not less than forty-eight hours; work assignments are to be changed to less desirable ones; and letters describing each incident will be placed in the inmate's file and with the parole examiner's file. There will be no exceptions. The Warden

The policy clarification is in response to increasing violence within the institution that has resulted in the injury of seven inmates and two officers during the month of July alone.

The memo is appropriate at this time because violence between inmates has escalated and needs to be curbed. It supports the staff because increased violence puts everyone at risk. You are happy that individual discretion has been removed; inmates can't blame you if they are put on report. The warden has mandated that a penalty is required, and you have no choice.

You are assigned to a dormitory unit that houses prison aides. Prison aides work irregular shifts, night shifts, or in the hospital; consequently, these inmates are often on call. They are presumed to be more trustworthy, which is why they are housed in the dormitory and have more flexible hours. Several of the inmates in this dormitory are administrative and one of them, Browning, probably typed the warden's memo on fighting.

You are working the graveyard shift, 11:00 PM to 7:00 AM. On Tuesday, shortly after midnight, you hear a disturbance and run immediately to the dormitory. From the corridor you turn on the overhead dorm lights. Inside, two inmates are crouched, ready for combat, on opposite sides of a single bed. Both are armed with sharp objects and are slashing at each other as they move from left to right around the

95

bed. The rest of the inmates, though reluctant to get involved, have now seen you. They are divided, with one group enjoying the diversion and wanting the action to continue, and the other group wanting to settle the fight. The combatants are also aware of your presence but continue to circle and glare. You quickly run to the end of the narrow corridor and call for help.

Returning to the dorm, you find that the inmates have returned to their respective beds and all weapons have disappeared. The confrontation is over. One of the men involved is an aggressive homosexual and former weight lifter who is the head baker for the staff dining room. The other person involved is the head clerk for the chief of prison security. Both offenders are eligible for parole in a few months.

You meet your lieutenant outside the dormitory and report: "Inmates Reynolds and Taylor were fighting, sir. They had weapons. I'll write up the report." The lieutenant ponders a moment. "Well, come on over to the office and let's talk about it." As you approach the office, the lieutenant says, "Look, Steve, you know nothing important happened. Let's not stick our necks out. It's hot. Arguments are bound to happen; it's over now. If you report this, these guys will be denied parole, and it'll mean grief for us all." You agree, but point out the recent directive on violence from the warden. "Well, do what you want," the lieutenant says, "but I advise against it."

If you do not report the incident, you will satisfy your lieutenant, who is your immediate supervisor. But if the warden learns of your failure to report the fight, the lieutenant probably will neither back you nor admit that he advised you to violate the directive. The warden will more than likely hear of the incident, since all of the inmates in the dormitory work for the administrative staff. Grapevine communication in the prison is quite active, and very little goes unnoticed. Also, the inmates who know of the directive will know that you deliberately violated a major policy. You worry about the example that sets and wonder if they will lose respect for you if you do not write up the incident. If you do write the report, it is sure to anger some of the inmates, particularly Browning, the clerk who types in the warden's office. Browning is the boyfriend of the weight lifter and would not want him to lose his job in the prison bakery. The civilian food-service manager will also be angry, since he will have to train a new bakery chef.

You believe that rules are necessary if there is to be order in the prison. You believe that directives, if legal, should be obeyed consistently and without reservation. If a directive is inappropriate, you believe that it should be challenged openly in a reasonable way. But you also feel that you must try to get along with the people you work with. You are the man in the middle. No matter what you do, you will upset someone. You must decide.

Questions for Discussion

The warden's new policy seems to be a good one, yet you stand to make a number of enemies if you proceed with the report. Should you make an exception in this case, since no one got hurt? What if the same two inmates have another confrontation and one of them is seriously injured? Should you then be held responsible, since you did not write up the initial incident?

Case 4

A Matter of Discretion

You are assigned as a correctional officer on Cell Block 12, a general-population wing in a maximum-security state prison. The inmates in your block all have assigned jobs and, for the most part, are pretty well behaved. On this particular night, Captain Stewart is the institutional watch commander for the third shift (evening watch, 3:00–11:00 PM). Everything has been quiet except for the occasional outbursts of shouting and applause in the inmate dayroom. The seventh and final game of the World Series is on television, and the inmates are avidly watching the hotly contested affair.

Suddenly you realize the time has slipped away as the bell rings, signaling it is "rack down" time—10:00 PM, lights out. As you enter the dayroom, inmates deluge you with requests to let them stay up until the game is over. It is the bottom of the ninth inning, two outs, a runner on third base, and the home team is down by one run.

You get on your walkie-talkie and radio the captain for advice, but he is unable to respond at the moment.

Questions for Discussion

The prison rules about "rack down" times are clear, and your watch commander is a stickler for following the rules. What should you do? Should you exercise your own best judgment and discretion, or should you "play it safe?"

Case 5

Elder Abuse

You have worked as a correctional officer on the midnight shift at the state prison for the past 3 years. It has been, at times, a rewarding job that you really enjoy. At other times, there have been incidents that continue to bother you. Your relationship with fellow officers is frequently strained, at best. As a college graduate, you are suspect to many of them. Senior officers have admonished you on a number of occasions to just "get along" and keep your personal views to yourself.

For the past 3 months, you have been assigned to the geriatric unit in the prison hospital. For the most part the nurses and officers are professional and treat the inmates with care. These are the most vulnerable inmates—old, infirm, many dying of various illnesses. Still others suffer from various stages of Alzheimer's or senile dementia. One elderly inmate has sleepless nights; he shouts nonsensically, cries out, and awakens other inmates with his outbursts. The man is supposed to be on continuous medication to help him sleep, but the nurse frequently withholds the sleeping pill. She and another officer on the shift have developed an obvious disliking for the old man. One night, immediately after he begins to cry out in his sleep, you start to go to his room, but the other officer tells you that he and the nurse will take care of it. Momentarily you hear the officer shouting at the old man, and then the inmate begins to cry out. After a few moments you decide to check on the continuing racket yourself. As you enter the inmate's room, you see the officer raising his right hand to strike the inmate. The officer has a belt in his hand, and before you can say or do anything, he strikes the inmate in the head with the belt buckle, screaming at him to "shut up." The nurse is holding the feeble old man down so he can offer no resistance.

When the officer and nurse notice you standing there, the officer tells you the bruises and marks around the old man's head are a result of him "falling out of bed." The officer glares at you as he instructs you to "mind your own business."

Questions for Discussion

What are some ways the prison administration and treatment staff could help you and other correctional officers feel more confident and better qualified to deal with such situations? Should these situations be reviewed by institution training staff to determine if officers are prepared to deal with such events?

Case 6

A Riot in the Making?

The correctional supervisor, Sergeant Jackson, is sitting in his cluttered office working a week-old crossword puzzle. Outside his window a black inmate in white coveralls works in the garden, snipping and raking, making sure that flower beds are just so. Across from the "Visiting Park," other inmates march toward work areas. A prison runner jogs down the brick street inside the walls; the 100-year-old live oaks that line the street stand motionless in the still afternoon heat. Elsewhere, the factory noises are beginning to resume following the noon break. The two-way radio crackles in his office, but unless someone calls his name he ignores it.

The Department of Corrections inspection team is scheduled to arrive this afternoon. They will be accompanied by two newspaper reporters. An ad hoc group of professional and civilian members of the Governor's Prison Reform Committee has been touring the grounds for the past few days, surveying the more glaring inadequacies of the institution and suggesting remedies where possible. Several dormitory units have been quickly painted. Trash has been removed and burned, and there has been a general shakedown and cleanup of cell blocks. Even a new dinner menu has been created to provide more substantial and satisfying meals for the inmates.

The inmates are aware of the impending visit. Some of the more militant ones have been protesting the cleanup on the grounds that the administration is trying to cover up the inadequacies of the institution. Showers, which are usually allowed only once weekly, have been increased to four times a week. Use of medication, such as tranquilizers, has been increased, and some of the inmates regarded as "difficult" have been removed to administrative segregation. Overcrowding is a serious problem, as is the quality and frequency of correctional officer training. Still, somehow the system has worked for the last 10 years.

Even though Sergeant Jackson's office is less than a showplace, he has straightened it. His clipboard rosters and administrative directives,

101

accumulated in reverse chronological order, hang from hooks instead of lying randomly on whatever flat spot is available. Even as he works his crossword puzzle, he keeps a wary lookout for premature or unexpected official visitors. "Sergeant Jackson," the radio interrupts, "Sergeant Jackson." The sergeant reaches over, grabs the standing mike, and keys it. "Yeah, Jackson here."

"This is Tolliver. I've got the makings of a problem here. A group from 'E' wing has set up a committee and they want to speak, as a group, to the inspection team this afternoon. I told them I didn't think this was possible, but I said that I would ask you."

"Come on! You know that group of clowns; all they want is a country club. Troublemakers, every one of them. Tell them to forget it!"

"They are pretty insistent, sir."

"You make sure to remind them that the inspectors are only going to be here for a few hours, but we'll be here tomorrow. Remind them how we handled the last inmate protest."

"Okay, I'll tell 'em, but I don't think they will listen."

Sergeant Jackson returned to his crossword puzzle, grumbling to himself about devious inmates always trying to get more than they deserved. Suddenly the radio came alive.

"Sergeant! Sergeant! A group of inmates are moving toward Central Control. They have pipes and appear to be holding three guards as hostages. Do you read?"

Sergeant Jackson grabbed the mike. "Yes, damn it. I read. How many are there? Exactly where are they? Do you have visual contact?" The voice on the other end failed to respond.

Sergeant Jackson looked up from his radio into the scowling faces of armed inmates. Central Control had been taken!

Questions for Discussion

How could Sergeant Jackson have reacted in a different way that might have defused the incident that led to seizing three guards and taking Central Control? What are some policies the prison administration could have developed to deal with inmate grievances and other institutional problems that might affect inmates?

Case 7

A Question of Policy

As a female correctional officer, you have been working at the same women's prison for 15 years. The inmates call you Marge and respect you as being firm yet fair. You have made some mistakes during your career, but no one has ever questioned your intentions or integrity. Like anyone working in a prison, you liked some inmates more than others. However, it is rare for you to find an inmate whom you cannot work with at all. In fact, you are dedicated to the point that you will often spend some of your own time participating with the female inmates in recreation, arts and crafts, and other cell-block activities.

There is one inmate of whom you are particularly fond. She is a young woman about 19 years of age incarcerated on a drug offense. Lisa is a shy girl who comes from a broken home. She never had much of a family life; both of her parents had failed in previous marriages. Lisa's drug problems had started in high school when she got mixed up with the wrong crowd. She felt accepted by the kids who used drugs, and it was easier to cope with life while on drugs. Lisa was just beginning to use hard drugs when she got busted. Because she was with a friend who was selling large quantities of drugs, her bust resulted in a trial and a 2-year sentence.

While in prison, Lisa has come to you on several occasions with personal problems. Being a first-time offender, she has found adjusting to prison life very difficult. You and she have become good friends in a mutually trusting relationship. On this particular day, however, your relationship has been tested.

Lisa has asked you to mail a personal letter to a close friend who lives in her home town. Since her friend is not a member of her family or her lawyer, his name is not on the approved mailing list. She knows your mailing the letter is a violation of institutional policy, but it is very important to her that she contact her friend just this one time. You know that other correctional officers occasionally mail letters for inmates. You also realize that it would be quite easy for you to mail this particular letter. Still, it is a violation of policy. If you do not mail the letter, your relationship with Lisa will more than likely deteriorate. If you do mail the letter, you may suffer consequences. The decision is going to be a difficult one.

Questions for Discussion

The inmate wants her correctional officer friend to mail a letter to someone who is not on the approved mailing list. What harm could such a small violation of policy possibly cause? Is knowledge about other officers occasionally mailing letters for inmates a relevant factor in Marge's decision? Should Marge discuss the policy with administrators to determine if an exception could be made to place a non-family member on the approved mailing list? Perhaps this could be a compromise where she doesn't break the rules but can still accommodate the request. Still, this could create the perception that she is lenient toward inmates, which could cause difficulties with fellow staff members and create a precedent for other inmates.

Case 8

Family Connections

You and another correctional officer, Terry Warner, supervise inmates working in the prison laundry during first shift. Philip Ashton, an inmate serving 30 years for multiple assaults, has pulled you aside and complained about Officer Warner.

Ashton is a brooding, tightly wound inmate who, while quiet and introverted most of the time, has exploded on occasion. Eight months ago he almost killed an inmate who questioned his manhood. During the morning break, he whispers to you that Officer Warner has been playing with a large pocket knife and occasionally taunts him and several other inmates when no one else is around. Policy dictates that the only weapon correctional officers can carry is their nightstick. You also notice that Ashton's hands are shaking when he tells you that if something isn't done, he is afraid of what he might do to the officer in question.

With 8 months until your retirement and a full pension, Philip Ashton's complaint is the last thing you want to deal with. Terry Warner is the kind of corrections officer that wouldn't have a job if his cousin was not the head of security. Major Art Warner is everything his bumbling, inept buffoon of a cousin isn't, but cousins are still cousins and, as the old saying goes: "Blood is thicker than water."

Questions for Discussion

The inmate has come to you. Should you report the incident to Major Warner? Will the major believe you or his cousin? Is there anything you can do to cover yourself?

SECTION V

The Counselor

Correctional counselors deal with the emotional climate of a correctional environment, attempting to provide inmates with adjustment and rehabilitation counseling services. These services may be rendered on an individual basis or in a group setting.

The introduction discusses the counseling process and treatment categories. The eight cases present a variety of professional and personal situations in which correctional counselors typically find themselves. Dealing with inmate depression, anger, and deception as well as with the counselor's own sense of frustration are examples of skills required of the correctional counselor. As you react to the cases, consider the feelings of the counselor and the inmate with whom he or she is working.

Introduction

Correctional or offender counseling involves a variety of helping professionals working with persons who have either informally or formally been identified as delinquent and/or criminal. Each offender presents the counselor with a unique counseling situation and challenge. In many instances, there may be little promise of an adequate resolution. The variety of experiences shape the counselor's professional attitude and style.

The idea of "correctional" counseling may not be compatible with the legitimate interests and purposes of helping offenders. For instance, is the primary goal of counselors who work in prisons one of correcting offenders for successful readjustment to the outside world, or is their primary role more concerned with offenders' adjustment to the institutional world of the prison? Does the basic goal of probation/parole counselors revolve around therapeutically correcting offenders under their supervision, or are they more concerned with case management and the enforcement of the conditions of probation/parole? More fundamentally, one might ask whether or not there is any substantial evidence that counselors can, in fact, "correct" offenders. What seems to be a more appropriate focus is to view counselors as helping professionals who attempt to apply their skills and expertise in correctional and related settings (Varghese, Fitzgerald, Chronister, Cummings, & Forrest, 2013). The primary goal of offender counselors and therapists appears to be one of intervening therapeutically with various clients, the majority of whom happen to be offenders. These interventions address multiple circumstances, including prison adjustment, pre- and post-release vocational and marital/family readjustment, and juvenile problems.

Most correctional counseling jobs are state and local government positions. Correctional counselors work with juvenile offenders, in community corrections (probation and parole), in jails, or in state and federal prisons. Education requirements for correctional treatment specialists vary by state (Sun, 2013). Most employers require a bachelor's degree. Generally, correctional agencies are looking for people who demonstrate a desire to work in corrections and a belief in the value of helping to rehabilitate offenders. In 2017, 87,700 people were employed as correctional treatment specialists and probation officers; about 46,000 worked for state governments and almost 39,000 for local governments (Bureau of Labor Statistics, 2018). The average wage was $56,630.

The Counseling Process

Offender counseling and psychotherapy, as with all clinical helping, comprises a process that includes three essential abilities: a sense of timing, effective risking, and a sense of professional humility.

Many counselors and psychotherapists, particularly those who work with offenders, may find it difficult to pay adequate attention to their clients' communication. To a large extent, the difficulty stems from the counselor's professional and personal attitudes that reflect the dual responsibility of security and treatment plus the retributive feelings of society in general. In other words, the offender counselor grew up in and came from a social system that is often oriented toward punishment. The counselor working in a correctional setting sets his or her priorities as follows: (1) the security/custody needs of the agency and community; (2) the treatment and rehabilitation needs of the offender.

For the counselor to develop a *sense of timing*, he or she must be able to assess clients as they are now versus categorizing them by their past behavior. Respecting and understanding where the client is now helps the counselor have a more accurate perception of the general condition of the offender, which facilitates implementing a meaningful treatment strategy. Empathic listening enables the counselor to build a relationship with his or her client—an essential component for increasing the potential for positive change. The ability to listen attentively to a client requires both patience and perseverance. Giving advice to a client before adequately understanding what they are trying to communicate is like a physician attempting to provide medical treatment before thoroughly assessing the nature of the patient's illness. Counselors should listen for cues to important feelings—what is said is sometimes less important than how and when it was said.

Effective risking is an important skill for offenders to learn. Taking risks is not new behavior for many offenders. They risked arrest and possible imprisonment when they committed crimes. Risking in a therapeutic sense, however, is different. Substantially changing one's attitude and behavior requires serious efforts and involves emotional risks for anyone. For those who have committed crimes, their offenses may have been symptoms of deeper conflicts. Problems that took a lifetime to evolve cannot be changed quickly. The key is to learn to take risks effectively. Some offenders act impulsively without thinking about possible consequences. The counselor can guide the client in assessing the potential costs of his or her actions.

When evaluating the potential costs of a particular risk, the counselor can use three questions to help the offender focus on responsibility: (1) Who am I? (2) Where am I going? and (3) Why? The first question is a catalyst for helping clients develop a better perspective on their past successes and failures, as well as their hopes for the future. There are two aspects to the second question: Where do I currently see myself? and Where do I hope to see myself in the future? This question is particularly relevant in helping offenders with risk taking regarding vocational and career decisions. The third question is useful in helping clients develop a greater sense of accountability for the choices they make and the risks they take. The individual can examine his or her priorities in depth and make a responsible decision.

Professional humility is the result of one's attitude and, perhaps, of life itself. Experience teaches us that life is not always fair, and we cannot always win. Life is paradoxical. Sometimes what seems to be right may, in fact, be wrong and what appears to be wrong may, in fact, be right. Right and wrong may differ simply in degree and be relative to a given context. The counselor cannot really correct a client any more than offenders can be assured that if they make positive, socially acceptable decisions, they will be treated fairly. What the counselor and client can both do is to attempt to make the most informed choice. The therapeutic context in which such choices can be made is relational.

Relationships form the basis for the therapeutic efforts of the counselor and offender. Trust is an essential component in relationships.

The offender will transfer both positive and negative feelings to the counselor as a part of the dynamics of the relationship process. How the counselor responds to these feelings will have a substantial impact on any potential attitude change on the part of the offender.

William R. Miller (1983) first developed motivational interviewing for use in counseling substance abusers. He wanted a means of evoking personal motivation for change that avoided the defensiveness that often resulted from a directive style of counseling. Motivational interviewing helps clients decide to make a positive change on their own instead of the solution being suggested by the counselor. The counselor structures conversations so that the client reflects on the advantages of changing their behavior instead of eliciting a denial of the problem (Miller & Rollnick, 2013). This technique has been shown to be effective among many different types of clients, including criminal offenders (McMurran, 2009).

The offender is likely experiencing some degree of conflict regarding whether to make a change or not. The job of the counselor is to guide clients in discovering their feelings—not to point out discrepancies. "People are more likely to be persuaded by what they hear themselves say" (Miller & Rollnick, 2013, p. 13) than by what someone else tells them about accepting an uncomfortable reality. If people are motivated to change their harmful behavior on their own, they develop self-confidence in their abilities and value the solution.

Part of therapeutic counseling is modeling the importance of putting attentions into action—*therapeutic intention*. Although there are no guarantees regarding the outcomes, perseverance is more important to long-term rehabilitation and stability than immediate results. The attempt itself is a meaningful reward, regardless of the final outcome. In the final analysis, the self-respect earned through trying to make appropriate choices may be the most important correctional benefit the criminal justice system can offer.

Types of Offender Counseling

Intervention by counseling professionals with a disruptive individual *before* they become officially designated as an offender by the criminal justice system is the optimum situation. Elementary and high school guidance counselors and teachers, in addition to youth camp counselors, are examples of helping professionals who can make a difference before, rather than after, an individual's official contact with the criminal justice system. For counselors who work with offenders in correctional settings, there are two general categories: community-based and institutional.

Community-based counselors include probation and parole service professionals and halfway-house counselors. Other secondary, yet very important, professional resources include mental health centers, employment agencies, volunteers, private helping centers (e.g., alcohol and drug counseling), and pastoral counselors or other church-related resources. Most offenders are treated at the community level, making each of these individuals critical to the success of the justice system.

Probation is utilized primarily as a means of diverting juvenile and adult offenders from correctional institutions. The probation officer/counselor is engaged in a variety of investigative services (e.g., supervision, furlough, work release, presentence, etc.) as well as providing counseling services. As discussed in section I, probation consists of sentencing an offender to a community-based treatment or other correctional program rather than incarcerating the individual. The alternative sentence is subject to certain judicial conditions, including having the offender supervised by the probation agency. Parole and probation officers are both involved in *revocation* proceedings—a process that responds to violations of the conditions of probation or parole by the offender and may involve reinstatement of incarceration.

There are conflicts inherent in the roles of both probation and parole officers. Probation/parole professionals are responsible for enforcing the conditions of probation or parole and for providing guidance services. The treatment versus security conflict centers on the issue of confidentiality. If the offender is aware that his or her probation/parole officer must investigate and enforce the conditions regarding probation or parole, how confidential a relationship would the client be willing to establish with the probation/parole officer? As mentioned previously, the relationship between the counselor and offender is fundamental to a successful outcome.

One common problem for probation officers is that they often have not been educated in counseling techniques. Thus, departments often need to train their officers to carry out their treatment role effectively. Many probation departments provide training on counseling techniques such as motivational interviewing. Research suggests that motivational interviewing is effective in helping clients initiate and maintain behavior change (Stohr & Walsh, 2018). For example, probation officers who use motivational interviewing have been found to be more effective at encouraging substance-abusing probationers to enter treatment programs (Spohr, Taxman, Rodriguez, & Walters, 2016). However, it must also be noted that not all probation officers have the skill or desire to engage in motivational interviewing (Viglione, Rudes, & Taxman, 2017). A department's priorities and organizational culture might also impact the extent to which probation officers are encouraged to counsel their clients. One supervisor specifically told a probation officer to spend less time with probationers and instead make sure that the paperwork was completed properly.

The creation of specialty probation caseloads for offenders with mental health issues is a relatively recent development. One of the many advantages to such a caseload is the ability to better train probation officers on mental health issues and proper counseling techniques for probationers in this category. One study found that probation officers who had a specific caseload of offenders with mental illness spent most of the time in meetings discussing the probationers' mental health, including the side effects of medication (Louden, Skeem, Camp, Vidal, & Peterson, 2012). While officers did ask questions pertaining to compliance with probation rules, less time was spent counseling on issues such as financial assistance, employment, or criminogenic attitudes. This caseload model has been found to foster higher-quality relationships between probation officers and probationers as well as result in better probationer outcomes (Epperson, Thompson, Lurigio, & Kim, 2017; Manchak, Skeem, Kennealy, & Louden, 2014). *Institutional-based* counselors include youth counselors in juvenile correctional institutions and counselors in male and female adult prisons. These counselors are badly needed, as a large percentage of inmates report mental health or drug abuse problems (Bronson & Berzofsky, 2017; Bronson, Stroop, Zimmer, & Berzofsky, 2017). Ironically, the philosophy of policy makers often includes removing offenders from relatively normal, law-abiding community environments to more abnormal, overcrowded, often isolated, institutional environments to help the offender learn to become law-abiding. The philosophy may satisfy the retributive inclinations of society but has not been successful in rehabilitating offenders. An important question to consider is: How long can our society afford the financial and human costs of this type of philosophy?

Most correctional facilities offer a variety of programs and activities designed to benefit inmates (Stephan, 2008). However, the proportion of service professionals providing rehabilitative services to inmates has declined since the 1980s, resulting in a more punitive correctional experience over this period of time (Phelps, 2012). To a large extent, institutional counselors are often more involved in institutional maintenance than in offender or correctional treatment. The primary concern of administrators, security officers, and treatment professionals alike is to insure that the prison environment remain manageable. This is not to suggest that treatment or rehabilitation never occur, but such goals are often secondary instead of primary.

Treatment Categories

In correctional institutions, there are three basic categories related to treatment: education, recreation, and counseling/casework. The *educational* specialist working in a prison or the correctional educator in general is confronted with a less than ideal population of potential students. As a group, offenders represent a substantial, if not profound, record of failure. Prisoners have much lower levels of education compared to the general population (Ewert & Wildhagen, 2011). Learning disabilities, negative attitudes, and scarce resources all contribute to a perpetuation of failure and underachievement that was experienced by offenders before incarceration. Traditional educational approaches simply do not work with most offenders. These persons represent the failures of the typical school environment.

In the general population, 20% fall below the literacy level compared to 39% in prison (Travis, 2011). Learning disabilities affect 6% of the general population and 17% of incarcerated individuals. Correctional populations have a wide range of levels of education—from almost total illiteracy to some postsecondary experience (Brazzell, Crayton, Mukamal, Solomon & Lindahl, 2009). A significant number of inmates have learning disabilities, behavioral problems, and/or mental health issues that complicate their educational needs. These issues are often undiagnosed or misdiagnosed. Students with an enormous range of skill levels are sometimes in the same classroom in correctional facilities. In addition to these challenges, facility policies/procedures restrict educational achievement (Mackenzie, 2012). Restricted movement in facilities, lockdowns, and transfers to other institutions limit classroom time. Security concerns prohibit Internet use, which reduces the ability of offenders to obtain information.

Recent studies indicate that 33% of adjudicated juveniles could be classified as learning disabled (Leone & Weinberg, 2012). Unfortunately, most incarcerated juveniles do not have access to the same level of educational services as the general population. Among states that do offer the same types of educational services, the programs are often not held to the same standards for accreditation as are traditional public schools (The Council of State Governments Justice Center, 2015). It is unlikely that a small staff of correctional counselors working with these children can make a significant positive impact. Instead, educational barriers must be addressed by collaboration between the various agencies that serve children in the community.

The lack of education, combined with the offenders' criminal record, makes finding a steady job increasingly difficult and might increase the likelihood of recidivism. Fortunately, correctional education can have an impact. Several recent studies have found that inmates participating in correctional education programs are significantly less likely to recidivate compared to inmates not receiving educational opportunities (Davis et al., 2014).

Although not always his or her primary responsibility, the educational specialist in prison may also be involved in vocational/career training and guidance. Vocational training helps reduce prison misconduct, helps inmates obtain better employment after release, and contributes to reduced recidivism (Duwe, 2017). The costs of such programs are far outweighed by reduced costs on correctional systems for rule infractions and less incarceration for new crimes. Gainfully employed ex-offenders pay taxes, generating revenue for state, and federal governments. The prevention of crime generates monetary benefits for society. For example, each dollar spent on educational programming by the Minnesota Department of Corrections generated $3.69 in cost-avoidance benefits.

Inmates working in vocational programs developed an improved perception of self, increased interpersonal skills, and a sense of pride in their work (Richmond, 2014). Further, the fear of losing their prison job created an incentive to stay out of trouble within the facility. Even in correctional institutions where vocational training resources are severely limited, education and counseling specialists can use prison work as training opportunities for offenders. For instance, counselors can work with the prison's food service division to implement baker, dietician, or other food-related training programs.

Education, whether it is of an academic or vocational nature, involves relationships. In situations that vary from motivating an offender through individualized educational instruction to helping an offender choose a vocation that is both meaningful and marketable, the relationship component cannot be underestimated. The counseling and other interpersonal skills modeled by the educator in his or her relationships with offenders are often critical in determining the margin of success or failure. The best of educational and vocational programs will not work without meaningful educator/offender relationships. Limited program resources can often be overcome as a result of dynamic, positive staff/offender relationships.

The *recreation* specialist in institutional corrections comprises a vital part of both the security and treatment process. Recreation has distinct advantages over other treatment programs. For instance, one does not have to be able to read and write in order to participate in and learn from recreational programs. Even physically disabled offenders can engage in a variety of recreational activities (e.g., arts and crafts, table games). A major problem regarding correctional recreation has been one of perception. Too often, the public views any sort of recreational program as coddling inmates. In particular, prison weight-lifting programs have received a great deal of media attention and political commentary among those who fear that prisoners are simply using taxpayer money to become more physically dangerous (Tepperman, 2014). Despite these concerns, many recreational programs exist in prisons, including various sports, weight lifting, and crafts. Prison officials generally support these programs, if for no other reason than the presence of a privilege that can be taken away for poor behavior (Delaney, 2016).

The treatment versus security dilemma is nowhere more evident than in the area of correctional recreation. If a correctional institution does *not* utilize a varied and comprehensive recreation program, inmates are left with a substantial amount of idle time and very few appropriate outlets to vent any frustrations or tensions they might be experiencing. The result can be an increase in physical and emotional conflicts ranging from assaults to personal depression. While recreation programs offer a number of advantages, they also create scheduling concerns. Inmate meals, work assignments, education programs, and other aspects of institutional life need to operate smoothly in conjunction with recreation activities. Another concern involves *supervision* of recreation events. Inadequate supervision could result in a security and treatment nightmare. Ineffective supervision of recreation programs would not only undermine the potential treatment value of such activities but could also result in increases in prison violence, escape attempts, and other counterproductive behaviors. As far as a correctional counselor is concerned, recreation may well comprise the most important treatment and maintenance component of a correctional institution's programming.

Whether one is an education or recreation specialist, effective counseling and interpersonal skills are critical. *Counseling/casework* provides a cohesiveness that enables institutional and other programmatic activities to run as smoothly as possible. Traditionally, counselors work with individual clients and also conduct group counseling sessions relating to different kinds of problems (e.g., drug abuse, sexual offenders, suicide prevention). Formally and informally, counselors function as crisis interveners. Interventions take place across a wide range of interpersonal situations—from the newly-arrived, first-time offender who is anxious and depressed to the inmate who has just been turned down for parole. Counselors are to some extent maintenance workers; they try to help offenders adjust to and function in the institution with a minimum amount of interpersonal frustration and damage. While effective treatment and rehabilitation does occur, they are often secondary to general crisis intervention and maintenance functions. Some offenders genuinely want to change, but others do not. Many offenders are comfortable with their criminal careers and engage in counseling as a means of improving their situation in prison and their chances for getting out as soon as possible.

Correctional counselors deal with involuntary clients; some are hostile and angry (Sun, 2013). Inmates are generally much more diverse than the counseling staff. Despite their required participation, offenders are just as motivated to understand their experiences as anyone else. "Competent counselors should be able to play an effective role in counseling multicultural clients, adhering to social justice, discerning the clients' true problems, selecting and implementing interventions, and reducing recidivism" (p. 2). Positive changes in social-cognitive capacity, motivation, emotional adjustments, relationship problems, or career planning help empower clients and give them tools to improve their lives.

Summary

Correctional counseling involves therapeutic intervention with offenders. The primary interventions include prison adjustment, pre- and post-release vocational and social readjustment, and juvenile problems. The effective correctional counselor must possess three essential abilities: a sense of timing, effective risk taking, and a sense of professional humility. Through modeling, the counselor guides the client to a belief that appropriate choices in life can be made.

The most important counseling is preventive in nature. Offender counselors have the greatest chance of preventing criminality before an offender becomes officially designated as an offender by the criminal justice system. Of the two basic types of correctional counseling (community-based and institutionally based), community-based correctional counseling appears to be the most effective. The nature and environment of correctional institutions often prohibit effective counseling to prepare an offender to return to society, emphasizing instead the maintenance of institutional security and coping within the institution.

There are three basic treatment categories in correctional institutions: education, recreation, and counseling/casework. Institutional education programs offer teacher-student relationships that may enhance an offender's ability to succeed on the outside. Recreation also involves relationships that show how the methods for successful participation in various games and activities can become skills useful after release—translating the "rules of the game" into "rules for living.". Counseling/casework involves crisis intervention help for offenders. The counselor, in this sense, is attempting to help the offender adjust to the institutional environment and other related interpersonal problems.

The effectiveness of correctional counseling depends on what is defined as effective. Some maintain that effective counseling is that which is the most economical and functional in terms of routine handling of offender-institutional problems. Others maintain that effective counseling is that which adequately prepares an offender for release into society. Effective correctional counseling includes: (1) a clear clinical/professional identity; (2) effective use of timing, risking, and humility in a helping sense; and (3) therapeutic intentions, where the helping attitude and efforts of the counselor may be more important than traditional measurements of success (e.g., recidivism rates).

Wet Behind the Ears

Four years at the university studying corrections and sociology have finally paid off. You have landed your first job as a correctional counselor in a medium-sized prison. Although you do not have any previous work experience, you were an A and B student in school and did especially well during your internship. After arranging your new office to your taste, you were ready to become a dynamic part of the rehabilitation process.

At the beginning of the work day you met with the other counselors and your supervisor for coffee and the day's caseload assignments. You were somewhat puzzled at the mixture of amused and disinterested stories that greeted your remarks on the latest research and theory concerning the practice of correctional counseling and treatment. As the day wore on, you became even more perplexed. The security officers escorting your inmate clients were always at least 15 minutes late. Two of your clients did not even come for counseling; one, who was illiterate, wanted you to read a letter for him from home, and another one wanted you to help him complete an order form for a leather-work kit. To make matters worse, you noticed that two of the other counselors worked with only one client each during the entire morning, while you saw four different clients. The two counselors spent most of their morning drinking coffee and "shooting the breeze" with each other in one of the offices.

After lunch everything seemed to slow down even more. You could not even get one of your scheduled clients in to see you at all. When you discussed the problem with the security officer responsible for escorting your client, he turned to you and replied, "I got more important things to do than to escort convicts all day." Then, without another word, he abruptly walked away before you even had a chance to reply.

Later that afternoon you had the chance to talk to two of the more experienced counselors, Ned and Julie. Julie had recently completed her master's degree in counseling. She was clearly hard working and ambitious. Her advice to you was succinct and to the point. "Do you want to become a burned-out malcontent like some of these other counselors, or do you want to get ahead? It's all in the paperwork. I do more case files than anyone else, and I constantly network with people who can help my career. You do the same and you will move right up the ladder of success. If you don't, you will be stuck here like the rest of them."

Ned, in his mid-50s, lit up his favorite pipe and propped his feet up on the table. He asked you about your family. Every time you mentioned one of the problems you had observed, he just smiled. As you got up to leave, he offered you some parting advice: "Luke, you need to lighten up a little, do what you can to help, and let the rest go. Give yourself a little more time on the job before you decide what's what."

The end of your first working week finds you tired and confused. Most of the other counselors don't seem to care about rehabilitation or any of the other things they were taught in college. They all have behavioral science degrees. What has happened to them? Will the same thing happen to you? Your supervisor also told you to take it easy and give the others a chance to get to know you. Is a career in corrections right for you, or was your choice a mistake?

Questions for Discussion

Are you experiencing the normal frustration of adjusting from the university to an actual work setting? Are you expecting too much, too soon? Are the more experienced counselors too complacent? Should you be more interested in career advancement, or can there be a balance between a career and simply helping?

Case 2

Confidentiality or Security?

You have been working as a counselor at the community correctional center for three years. You feel good about your job and the results you have achieved. No inmate or civilian has ever questioned your ethics or integrity.

You are presently working on an especially interesting case. A 22-year-old, second-time drug offender named Ted has really been opening up to you and seems to be turning himself around in terms of his personal values and motivation. The trust between the two of you is apparent. In fact, just several days ago the superintendent commented on how much better your client seemed to be doing since you had taken him on your caseload. However, during the last counseling session your client disclosed something that could severely disrupt your relationship with him, and you are not sure what to do about it.

Halfway through your last session, in a moment of frustration, Ted blurted the whole thing out. Apparently he and two other inmates had been planning an escape for some time. After Ted became your client and began making progress, he had second thoughts about being involved in the escape. The other two inmates, however, threatened to implicate him if anything went wrong with their attempt. The escape attempt is planned for tomorrow night. Ted is distraught as to what he should do—and now you are also distraught.

As a correctional counselor, you are not only responsible for counseling inmates but have implicit security responsibilities as well. If the escape attempt is allowed to continue as planned, correctional officers, inmates, or both might be seriously injured or killed. If you report the plan, you will have violated the confidentiality of your client, and Ted will most probably suffer repercussions. Needless to say, your counseling relationship with him will also be severely damaged. It seems you have to sacrifice both Ted and your counseling relationship with him or the security of the correctional center. Confidentiality or security, which must it be? Can there be another way?

Questions for Discussion

Should you inform Ted that you are professionally bound to tell the superintendent about the escape plans, while still attempting to work with Ted? Should you remain silent, hoping that the escape attempt will be unsuccessful and that no one will be injured? Should you go to the superintendent and discreetly attempt to thwart the escape attempt without letting Ted know of your actions?

Case 3

A Captive Audience?

You have been assigned as the head chaplain at a large state prison for men. One of your many duties is to coordinate a busy schedule of religious programs and activities. You have many lay volunteers who willingly give their time to provide religious programming to the nearly 2,000 men who are incarcerated there. Over the years you have developed and refined an excellent orientation and in-service training regimen for the lay volunteers. While you value their generosity, commitment, and enthusiasm, you also know that well-intentioned but naïve people can be easily manipulated by inmates. On the other hand, you are also mindful of your obligation to look out for the religious needs and best interests of the inmates as well. The fervor and tenacity of a few lay volunteers can become problematic. While you want dedicated and enthusiastic volunteers, you do not want people who are blindly driven to convert others to their way of thinking. Inmates are, after all, captive audiences.

These concerns always lead you to caution religious volunteers against pressuring inmates to participate in services or study classes or to be baptized into, join, or otherwise become actively engaged in any particular religious program. This direct and frank approach has always seemed to work well until now. You were called to the warden's office this morning and told that the governor's office had received complaints from several volunteers that you were discriminating against their church group and discouraging inmates from participating in their programs. The governor's directive is clear—stop messing with these fine people!

Questions for Discussion

While most church and religious groups work effectively within prison rules, this particular group has been a problem on a number of occasions, with inmates complaining about their "high pressure" tactics. How do you accommodate the governor's instructions yet still protect the inmates from unwanted intrusions?

Case 4

The Group

Ever since you earned your master's degree in social work, you have focused your counseling interests and skills on the group process. You even had a couple of articles published describing your group counseling efforts at the community-based halfway house where you are presently employed. Group work, in your opinion, is the best way to help people solve their problems. It is economical and efficient; you can see ten clients in a group during an hour, while in individual counseling you can see only one person at a time. Of course, you realize that individual counseling is necessary at times. Nevertheless, the group approach is usually better because it requires the group members to interact with each other rather than only with the counselor.

You have utilized the encounter-group process quite effectively on several occasions in the past with juvenile drug offenders. Confrontation seems to be particularly effective in dealing with the "conning" behaviors of many drug users. This approach also seems well suited to your personality as a therapist; no one has ever accused you of being nonassertive when dealing with a client.

Working with your most recent group, however, is proving to be a perplexing and frustrating experience. What began as a typical group of juvenile offenders engaged in open confrontation has degenerated into intimidation and thinly disguised threats. You have even heard rumors that some threats are being made outside the group. You realize you are losing control of the group but are not sure what to do about it. Now you have heard that two of the prison gangs who have members in the group have exchanged unpleasantries over what was said during one of the meetings. At the same time, two or three of the group members have made a lot of progress in accepting responsibility for their problems.

You do not want to admit defeat; you have never lost a group. Yet, confidentiality and adhering to the group's ground rules are essential to maintain trust. You are going to schedule one more meeting in an effort to clear the air and get the group back on track. What will you say? What will you do?

Questions for Discussion

What are your options in this situation? While you are concerned about the needs of the group members, does some concern about your own "track record" enter into the equation?

Case 5

The Despairing Client

Hector has been in prison for two years. He is a likable inmate who works in the prison library. He has a remarkable talent for repairing damaged books and has saved the library hundreds of dollars with his handiwork.

As his counselor, you try to see him at least once a month to find out how he is getting along. He always indicates that he is doing all right and that he is optimistic regarding his parole hearing, which is only nine months away. Hector has some reason to feel good about his chances for making parole. He is a first-time offender who got into a drunken brawl at a tavern and seriously injured another man. As a result of the altercation, he was sentenced to six years in the state penitentiary. Although Hector had experienced severe drinking problems for a number of years, fighting had never been a part of the problem. Since being in prison, he has joined Alcoholics Anonymous and even successfully completed several college-level courses in library science. Needless to say, counseling Hector is a pleasant experience mostly because of his motivation.

However, in the last several weeks Hector's behavior and attitude have changed. His wife, who has been visiting him faithfully every Sunday, has not shown up for the last two visitation days. Cell-house rumor is that she has begun seeing another man and is planning to file for a divorce. To make matters worse, the man she is involved with is an alcoholic himself. Hector has quit coming to work and keeps to himself in the cell house. He has also been losing weight and looks haggard and distraught.

As his counselor you want to help, but Hector, who has always been quiet, has now become even more withdrawn. You are not sure how to approach him. You have considered talking to his wife or his parents. If Hector's depression continues to worsen, his behavior may become unpredictable. He might become aggressive and get into a fight with someone in the cell house, or he might turn his anger inward and attempt suicide. You have to approach him, but how? You have to do something in an attempt to help him, but what?

Questions for Discussion

Hector's wife's decision to sue for divorce has affected him adversely. You want to help him, but is this possible? Can you help bring Hector and his wife back together? Can you help him reconcile himself to his wife's decision? What could you have done before the problems escalated into a divorce situation?

Case 6

Dealing with Anger

You have been a counselor for 10 years, but this is one part of your job that has never gotten any easier. Doug, an inmate at the institution where you work, has just been turned down for parole for the second time in six years. The two of you are sitting at the hearing-room table, quietly staring out the barred window. You can see the tears of frustration streaming down Doug's face. You can sense the anger and humiliation he is feeling and the explosion within himself that he is fighting to contain.

Doug has a good prison record with respect to both his conduct and his commitment to rehabilitation programs. The problem is apparently a political one. The local judge simply does not want Doug released in his county and lobbied the parole board to deny the request. As the institutional counselor, you know of several other inmates who have been granted parole to that particular county. They were paroled despite their having committed more serious offenses than Doug and having been much less receptive to the various institutional rehabilitation programs. Doug also knows of these paroles. To make matters worse, the parole board did not even give him a reason for rejecting his application, nor did they tell him what he could do to increase his chances for parole in the future.

Doug spent weeks in preparation for his parole hearing. The letters of recommendation, the acquisition of his high school diploma, and other related material had in the end meant nothing. The board had convened less than 10 minutes to make a parole decision based on six years of Doug's life. The chairman simply told you that Doug's parole had been denied and for you to pass the decision along to Doug. You had reluctantly done so, knowing that Doug could see the decision in your eyes before you even spoke. So here the two of you sit, bitter and disillusioned.

Will Doug give up? Will his anger get him into trouble with the administration or other inmates in the cell house? How will this affect your relationship with him, since you were the one who encouraged him to apply? You are not sure what to do or say, but somehow you have to try to help Doug pick up the pieces.

Questions for Discussion

Even though the parole denial in this particular case might have been politically motivated, how could the hearing have been better handled? Is there anything else you can do that might improve Doug's chances at the next hearing?

Case 7

Counseling a Hostage Victim

"Doc, I've been a corrections officer for 15 years. I've always looked forward to coming to work. But since I was taken hostage eight weeks ago, I'm not sure I can do my job anymore. I'm ashamed to admit it, but I'm afraid. I know me, Buddy, and Donny were only held by the inmates in C block for 48 hours, but I've been having problems ever since."

As the prison psychologist and a licensed therapist, you assure Frank that you understand and encourage him to continue.

"The thing that bothers me the most was seeing that young inmate raped by those three sons-of-bitches and not being able to help him. Every time I think about i. . . ." Frank stops talking and bows his head, quickly wiping a tear from the corner of his eye.

"Frank, go ahead. Let your feelings out. I would have been angry and scared, too. It's a tough thing to have to go through," you reply.

"Doc, it's worse than tough. Good lord, that young man is only 23 with a wife and baby. I haven't had a good night's sleep since this thing happened. And Buddy and Donny's done quit. Buddy's wife doesn't even know where he is. I want to go back to work, but my wife says I should quit and find something safer to do. The only thing I have ever done is corrections. I just don't know what to do. What do you think I should do, Doc?"

You look thoughtfully at Frank and rub your chin, wondering how you should respond. He needs to face his fears, but he and his family also need to have a life again. Frank is waiting for your opinion.

Questions for Discussion

Being the victim of a hostage incident can be very traumatic. Whether a correctional officer or an inmate, witnessing a rape or being raped is very disturbing and frightening. What are some relationship problems Frank may be experiencing? What are some different options within the prison that could ease Frank back into his work routine? Should his wife be included in your counseling sessions with him? Should he be referred to outside mental health professionals? Does the prison have an employee assistance program in place to deal with such situations?

Case 8

Suicide by Counselor

Your institution has a treatment program for inmates who are identified as sexual predators. Once identified, these inmates are placed in isolation in a maximum-security setting for 90 days. If they incur no disciplinary violations during that time, they are reviewed by the classification team and are eligible for release back into the general population.

Inmate George Nelson received a rule violation for breaking prison rules regarding unacceptable sexual behavior. Nelson has served his 90 days in isolation without receiving any write-ups for rules infractions. When he meets the classification committee, he is approved for release back into the general population. However, his caseworker, who works in an office next to yours, decided to leave him in isolation because she personally dislikes him. Five days later, after repeated unsuccessful requests to see his caseworker, Nelson hangs himself in his cell. He leaves a note saying he can't understand why he's not being allowed to get out of isolation. The deputy superintendent in charge of treatment is meeting with each of the caseworkers to investigate the note and circumstances surrounding George Nelson's death. You are scheduled to meet with the deputy warden first thing in the morning.

Questions for Discussion

Was this tragedy avoidable? Did George Nelson's caseworker act ethically or professionally? What are you going to tell the deputy superintendent when you meet with him? What do you think the outcome of this situation should be?

SECTION VI

The Correctional Administrator

The effective correctional administrator, whether in a community or an institutional setting, must possess significant management, leadership, and interpersonal skills. The introduction covers some of the basics of correctional administration. The seven cases offer a sampling of problems you might expect as a correctional administrator. Being a female superintendent of a women's prison, dealing with political pressures from within and without the correctional agency, and addressing prison sexuality are a few of the topics you will analyze in this section.

Introduction

Correctional administrators have a diverse range of responsibilities that must be managed ethically while complying with legal guidelines. First, administrators must maintain a safe and orderly facility for both inmates and correctional staff. They are accountable for preparing inmates for reentry to society, providing adequate food and medical care in the institution, developing and implementing effective human resource policies, supervising incoming and outgoing mail, and operating a commissary. This all must be done within increasingly tight budgets. As corrections consumed larger and larger shares of local and state government budgets, administrators found that outside scrutiny increased commensurately. The responsibilities of correctional administrators expanded from managing the institution to becoming an advocate for the institution's funding needs.

Successful administrators must use effective leadership skills to balance competing demands. It is not difficult to imagine that there are often contradictory goals among various departments in the institution. Correctional officers, treatment staff, and medical staff, will each advocate for

131

policies that make their work easier. Union contracts may contain clauses that counteract disciplinary proceedings for staff misconduct. Administrators need to create an organizational culture that emphasizes professionalism, striving to meet high standards, ethical behavior, positive interactions with inmates, and rewards for excellent work (Seiter, 2017).

The responsibilities of correctional administrators are influenced by public attitudes and by correctional philosophies. For example, the medical model of managing inmates during the rehabilitative era (1960–1980) emphasized diagnosing and treating the symptoms that caused criminality (Seiter, 2017). When a meta-analysis of research on the effectiveness of correctional treatment programs in reducing recidivism seemingly found that "nothing works," public officials no longer supported the medical model. Funding for rehabilitation declined, and several states eliminated parole. Judicial discretion was limited through mandatory minimums; longer sentences filled the prisons. Administrators were careful to avoid even minimal risks. Postgraduate degrees to obtain positions and/or to advance a career changed from social work to public administration. Despite the emphasis on custody, there was never a complete withdrawal of support for rehabilitation. Current philosophy emphasizes reentry and cost effectiveness. New data illustrates that rehabilitative programs can reduce recidivism and save governments money.

Correctional administrators face a series of challenging tasks in planning, organizing, and staffing to meet both treatment and custody goals for corrections. What are the goals? How should the work be divided? What departments will be in charge of what activities? Figure 1 depicts a typical organizational chart of a maximum-security prison facility. Corrections is organized along paramilitary lines, so the chain of command is clearly established. However, for effective outcomes, all levels of supervision must be aware of what others are doing (Seiter, 2017).

Upper-level administrators determine policy regarding the activities to be accomplished (Seiter, 2017). Mid-level managers create the procedures for implementing policies. Supervisors instruct employees in performing their duties. Policies and procedures should be clearly written; effective communication among management, supervision, and staff is essential for implementing the procedures and for establishing responsibilities. Staffing is another critical responsibility—hiring competent people, training them to complete their duties successfully, and assigning them to departments that fit their qualifications.

Social and Political Influences

Social attitudes play an important role in correctional policy. These social attitudes are influenced substantially by economics. During

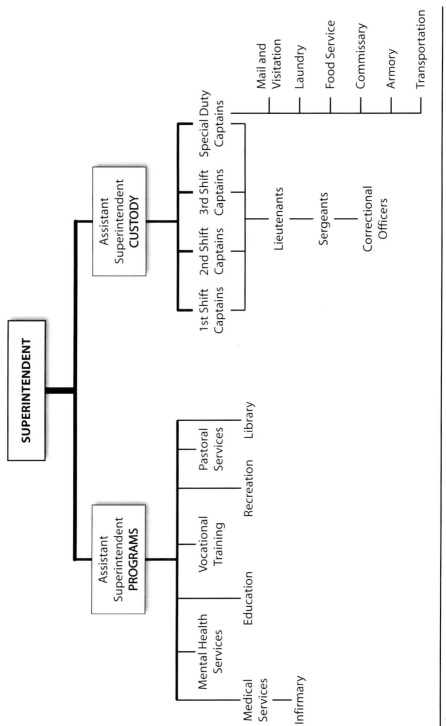

Figure 1 Organizational Chart

times of economic growth, public attitudes tend to support social treatment and services. When the economy is poor, public attitudes tend to reflect more conservative beliefs. During the 1960s, many entitlement programs and social services were made available based on public demands and concerns (e.g., social welfare, poverty, Social Security, Medicare, Medicaid, health and safety programs, etc.).

During that time of economic stability, court decisions about law enforcement and corrections protected the civil rights of the accused and incarcerated; reflecting the social attitudes of the time. As the economy deteriorated in the late 1970s, public attitudes became more conservative, increasingly favoring punishment and deterrence over the treatment of offenders. In the 1980s and 1990s a rise in media attention to crime issues fueled the public's desire for more punitive sanctions toward offenders. Televised court proceedings, police documentaries, and "most wanted" shows coupled with the public's frustration with the criminal justice system created public demands for harsher punishments (Kappeler & Potter, 2018; Surette, 2015).

Until 1980, corrections was a small part of state and federal budgets. Elected officials paid little attention to correctional operations. Prison security, community supervision, and rehabilitative programs were decided by the correctional administrator. Expenditures on corrections grew from $7.9 billion in 1981 to more than $52 billion (Seiter, 2017). Today, "every branch of government is involved in correctional policies and operations" (p. 42). The executive branch seeks accountability and cost savings, and the legislative branch passes statutes that affect administrative decisions. The courts adjudicate claims about whether correctional policies and operations are constitutional; in some cases the court appoints people to oversee operations.

To influence public policy, correctional administrators must manage the external environment, which includes elected officials, the media, social service agencies, and interest groups from victims to offender families. "The external environment is the arena in which philosophy around correctional issues is turned into public policy (Seiter, 2017, p. 56). Administrators must educate themselves about public opinion so that programs accommodate the interests of constituents and political leaders. This may involve compromise to incorporate positions important to others. "Failure to confront political realities by correctional administrators can result in public policy not supported by the experience and judgment of correctional professionals" (p. 280).

External issues are time consuming, whether reactive or proactive. Administrators must react to incidents at the institution that are reported by the media, such as an escape, a riot, or a violent crime committed by a parolee. Administrators must be proactive in educating elected officials and the public about the benefits of a desired change in policy. They can speak to community groups, grant interviews with the media, issue press releases about new programs, and testify at legislative hearings. The external contacts increase understanding about what corrections does.

Correctional administrators must be good salespersons, be knowledgeable about and proficient at public-relations, and be skilled in justifying large maintenance and treatment budgets to superiors, legislators, and the public (Jacobs & Olitsky, 2012). Treatment for offenders is expensive because it requires meaningful programs, equipment, and well-trained, qualified personnel. Legislators are inclined to favor more short-term, cost-effective efforts. However, specific treatment programs may require long-term measurement to determine effectiveness. It is often difficult for politically minded legislators and governors to make expensive commitments to correctional treatment when custodial care is much more economical for short-term measurement, not to mention pro-punishment public opinion.

The United States appears to have entered what Michael Tonry (2013) calls a stage of "equilibrium" where some of the most punitive policies from the 1980s and 1990s have been revised, and some innovations are starting to take hold as alternatives to prison. Economics, politics, and culture vary across regions and localities within the United States, which affects attitudes (Shannon & Uggen, 2012). Because large numbers of prisoners are released, there has been increased emphasis on programs to reduce recidivism, which is costly. The strain on budgets has contributed to the implementation of more cost effective programs.

Correctional Traditions and Fragmentation

Social institutions often embody traditions that lend strength and stability during times of change—but can also inhibit flexibility and the ability to change. Of all government institutions, corrections may be most bound by tradition. A good example is the litigation that has challenged correctional administrators over the past few decades. Administrators who have chosen to ignore prisoners' claims about rights violations have been deluged with lawsuits.

Historically, leadership in corrections has been based on the position occupied in the chain of command (Seiter, 2017). People in the highest positions make decisions, give orders, and reward followers for doing their jobs. If an issue surfaces that has not yet been addressed, people wait for superiors to tell them what to do. To succeed in such an environment, many employees model their behavior on that of their superiors, which strengthens tradition within corrections. Employees become institutionalized within the bureaucracy. If they are promoted, it is under a status-quo model. Planning in the traditional correctional management context was primarily tactical; if a problem arose, administrators would decide what tactics to use to address it. There were few attempts to think beyond the status quo—to make strategic, long-range plans that anticipate future needs. Correctional leaders need to change the culture if they want to implement innovative solutions. Leaders, managers, and staff need to work together to share their experiences to become more proactive rather than reactive.

Effective correctional administrators should also work toward overcoming the fragmented nature of the correctional process. Offenders need continuity of treatment and services as they transition from the judicial process of adjudication to various correctional environments and then back into society. Probation is often controlled by one system of corrections, parole another, juveniles another, and so on. Beginning in the early 2000s, states developed reentry programs that seek to integrate prison treatment and educational programming with community-based probation officers, employers, and treatment providers (Burke, Herman, Stroker, & Giguere, 2010). Correctional administrators need to realize that they can control only a small portion of the entire treatment program for offenders. However, working toward the goal of increased integration of each treatment component could benefit the inmates as well as help justify requests for increased budgetary allotments.

Correctional Management

There are many sociological and psychological theories for correctional treatment, most of which have been applied in one manner or another in corrections (e.g., individual therapy, group therapy, counseling, social work, psychological measurement, etc.). If any measurable success in offender rehabilitation is to be found in closed correctional facilities, the line workers and administrators will have to be adequately trained in and practice therapeutic methods as an integrated whole. Crisis problems of violence and suicide that exist outside the walls are exacerbated by the physical and social structure of a prison facility Police officers have found that training in crisis intervention skills helps prevent more serious conflicts from erupting (Edwards & Pealer, 2018). The same skills are required of correctional officers and administrators in what is a more potentially explosive environment.

Correctional administrators should not rely entirely on treatment personnel to handle therapy with inmates. Policies and procedures developed by administrators should follow an integrated treatment approach, including training of line workers in crisis intervention and counseling techniques. Too many correctional institutions seem split between administrative and line workers who lean more toward punishment methods and the counseling personnel who lean more toward treatment methods. With proper correctional management, many serious conflicts and incidents of violence may be prevented in closed correctional institutions.

All too often, correctional administrators find themselves involved in management by crisis—solving each problem as it arises without taking into consideration the long-range implications of the solutions and without seeking means by which the problem can be permanently eliminated. The administrator has a number of means available that he/she can use to monitor and control the prison operation. These include reports, records, and frequent evaluations. For example, an increase in the number of disciplinary reports may indicate to an alert administrator that prisoner dissatisfaction is increasing. The administrator's evaluation of the situation may point to inadequate food service, poor supervisory procedures, or to some new and unpopular administrative procedure. If the cause is isolated and analyzed quickly, it is possible to find an effective solution before it escalates.

A major issue facing correctional facility administrators is the supervision of special populations. For example, the combination of longer sentences, the change from indeterminate to determinate sentencing structures, and the increased age of newly sentenced offenders have contributed to the aging of the prison population (Carson & Sabol, 2016; Scaggs & Bales, 2015). This is expected to become an increasingly difficult problem for administrators as 1 in 7 prisoners are currently serving life sentences (Nellis, 2017). Older prison inmates face many more health-related problems than other inmate populations (Nowotny, Cepeda, James-Hawkins, & Boardman, 2016), resulting in significantly increased health-care costs. Aging inmates struggle with basic infirmities compounded by life in prison such as the susceptibility to cold temperatures, the ability to climb stairs or walk long distances without assistance, being assigned to upper bunks, and insufficient time to eat and shower (Leigey, 2015). Even serious disabilities experienced by elderly prisoners are often not recognized by the correctional officers and/or medical treatment personnel (Williams et al., 2009). Thus, correctional administrators may be unaware of the extent of difficulty experienced by their elderly population.

With the increased number of elderly prisoners serving life sentences comes the inevitability that states will continue to see a rise in inmates who die from natural causes within correctional facilities (Noonan, 2016). Prisons are generally ill equipped to handle end of life care. Security concerns, budgetary constraints, and lack of familiarity with best practices have all been identified by prison administrators as barriers to providing quality care to those nearing death (Penrod, Loeb, & Smith, 2014). In response to these challenges, many states have developed hospice care programs that specialize in the treatment of inmates with terminal diagnoses. Along with treating the inmate with a team of trained treatment specialists and volunteers, these hospice units also provide pastoral care and more lenient visitation policies to provide support for the inmate (Hoffman & Dickinson, 2011). One limitation to existing prison hospice programs is their relatively small size. These units will eventually need to be expanded as the prison population continues to age.

As society continues to demand punitive responses to sex offenders, this population has increasingly been sentenced to serve periods of incarceration. Sex offenders are considered a vulnerable population within the prison system due to their likelihood of being attacked by other inmates. In fact, a recent report showed that nearly 30% of the homicide victims inside California's prisoners were sex offenders (Thompson, 2015). From an administration perspective, few options are available to minimize the potential for violence. One common solution is to place the sex offender inmate in a segregation environment for their own protection. However, this option reduces the inmate's social interaction and treatment options, which could result in psychological distress. Since most of these inmates ultimately return to society, one could question the long-term impact on society if administrative segregation is overused. It is common for prisons to offer some sort of sex offender treatment programming. However, many inmates fear that their voluntary participation in such treatment will subject them to indefinite civil commitment following the completion of their prison sentence (Miller, 2010; Zoukis, 2017). This fear causes many sex offenders to refuse treatment and ultimately undermines the prison's ability to rehabilitate the offender.

The changing demographics of prison inmates are yet another example of how administrators must adjust to social and political forces outside of their control. Our social values and correctional theories have been ambivalent about what should be done with, to, and for criminals. Given such a state of ambivalence, correctional administrators may experiment with a variety of innovative methods of management and treatment without exceeding the boundaries of acceptable correctional administration. Correctional organizations are typically structured to resist change; any experimentation with innovation must be done slowly, with discretion, and careful consideration of various interest groups (e.g., correctional officers, treatment staff, elected officials, inmates, victims, and the public).

Summary

Correctional administrators have found in the last few decades that punishment and treatment must accommodate current social values and attitudes. Administrators must formulate policies and procedures that protect public interests and safety, which may mean compromising some aspects of their correctional policies. Administrators must be able to cope with social and political influences on correctional ideologies and recognize that the correctional process is fragmented, with only a small part of the process under their control. Historically, administrators adhered to traditional methods of correctional management. Today, they are answerable to legislators, the public, and the courts for their correctional policies.

Running a correctional institution is not an easy task, and the job is becoming even more complex Never has the correctional institution—and its administrator—been so visible to the public. And never has the correctional institution contained as many paradoxes and problems as it does today. The correctional administrator must continually struggle with the problems of conflicting priorities, limited funds, deficient facilities, and a limited staff. At the same time, the administrator is expected to find ways to develop his/her institution as a progressive, innovative correctional system sensitive to social needs and values and flexible enough to change and improve along with society.

Case 1

Anyone Want a Job?

The community college has been a good place to teach, but for the third year in a row there have been no pay raises for faculty and staff. This means that what started out as a decent entry-level teaching position in criminal justice is now a touch-and-go situation. Twenty-eight thousand dollars for a nine-month position, teaching four courses with 30 to 40 students each (plus field trips), the Criminal Justice Association, and the 30-mile commute have taken their toll. Now, with a new baby in the family and a 3% inflation rate each year, things are too tight for comfort. You need another job.

On your last visit to the Southeastern State Women's Correctional Institution with your students, you pointed out a list of jobs posted outside the prison. You always show your students these lists to demonstrate the monetary value of their college education, i.e., approximately $12 an hour with a GED or high school education, $14 with a 2-year degree, and $20 with a 4-year degree.

At the bottom of the list, you have repeatedly seen: "Training Director, $39–44,000." Although the pay seemed excellent, you had not been interested because you were happy in your current job. However, another year without a pay raise has resulted in you being more than interested. A call to the personnel office at the penitentiary is encouraging; they are very interested. You meet the state requirements of U.S. citizenship, age, and a felony-free record, 5 years experience in teaching or training, and a master's degree in education or criminal justice. You also have the ability to organize and manage prisoner and staff training programs, which is also a requirement. One of the hidden advantages not in the advertisement is that there is housing on the prison grounds and all the help one needs with domestic chores, not to mention the pay increase of at least $10,000.

Your resume looks impressive. You have a paragraph to cover each mandatory qualification including your three years as a drill sergeant in the army military police, your two years working in the county jail while in college, and your three years teaching at the community college in which you administered every aspect of the community college educational process for your 44 criminal justice students. You are also familiar with the surrounding educational institutions from which you graduated and maintain close contact with the faculty, an ideal situation for getting resources for staff development programs. Further, the vocational-technical school director at the community college had, in the past, expressed to you an interest in setting up some pre-release training at the penitentiary if an opportunity to do so ever presented itself. Finally, you often teach about the special needs of female prisoners, which you feel does not receive enough attention from lawmakers.

You were pleased with your application and resume when you submitted them to the state's central personnel office. If the central personnel board finds you qualified, they will put your name on the list and forward it to the Southeastern State Correctional Institution where the vacancy exists, and you could be interviewed in a matter of one or two weeks. You began to tie up some loose ends at the community college, trying not to be obvious. You hope to be employed elsewhere in the near future, and to renew some old ties at the nearby state university from which you graduated. When the letter finally arrived from the State Personnel Office, you were shocked to read that the advertised vacancy had been withdrawn because of "a lack of qualified applicants." You were invited to reapply if and when the search reopened. Could it be that the job was being held for someone else?

Your talk with the personnel officer at the correctional facility confirmed your worst fears. There had not been many applications, and you were viewed as the most qualified applicant by most of the search committee. However, the question arose of whether a man should be employed at a women's prison. Many of the inmates had been subjected to abuse by male figures in their past, and the prison did not want to trigger any negative emotions from the inmates. Further, the facility did not want the liability associated with a woman possibly accusing you of sexual misconduct. The personnel officer noted that while state law prevented them from discriminating based on gender in accepting applications, they had a practice of not hiring men in that facility. The position still exists and is currently unfilled, but funding to support it may be moved elsewhere to fill another budgetary need. You really want the position, but what can you do?

Questions for Discussion

How can you pursue the position? Should you contact the state senator from your district and ask for his help? Could you file a lawsuit in federal court, claiming that you have not been given an equal opportunity to compete for a state job for which you are qualified? Will either of these options risk the community college finding out that you are looking for another job? Perhaps there are other options. What will your next move be?

Case 2

Who's Running the Prison?

You came to the state correctional system with good credentials: an ex-military officer with 15 years in high-level correctional management positions and a recently completed master's degree in criminal justice. You are well qualified for almost any correctional-related position. You have a practical, no-nonsense attitude and feel quite comfortable in your new position as superintendent of the state penitentiary, which had been suffering from incompetent leadership and political intrigue.

The facility is in the state's most isolated corner, and the inmates there either are considered to have little potential for rehabilitation or were serving such long-term sentences that rehabilitation was of little immediate interest. In accepting the job as superintendent, you stated that your top priorities were to upgrade conditions in the prison, especially the physical plant, and to improve the quality of the correctional officer staff. Recently the two problems have become entwined in an unexpected way.

You had only been on the job for one week when the county commissioner for the district in which your institution is located came to see you. The commissioner, as you soon learned, was a political power in the county and could make conditions miserable for you if he wanted to. His son-in-law needed a job, and he wanted you to find a place for him on your staff. The discussion became heated, and before you knew it you said, "Hell no! I won't hire anybody unless they are qualified." The county commissioner left angrily.

A day later Senator Nester called. Senator Nester was on the state corrections committee and represented the district in which your institution was located. At the time he called you, you did not know that he was also on the appropriations committee. You learned later that if someone wanted a management job at the institution, he had to call Senator Nester in order to be hired. Senator Nester said in his call that he wanted to "get acquainted" and give you a little friendly advice.

First, he indicated that you should make a serious effort to get along with all the local officials. Second, he recommended that you hire the county commissioner's son-in-law. You told the senator that you would look at the son-in-law's application when he submitted it, and if he was qualified, you would give him serious consideration, but beyond that you could make no promises.

Your review of the son-in-law's hastily submitted application revealed that he had a high school diploma, had been a police officer on a local force, and had held several other unrelated jobs—all of rather short duration. In short, he might be qualified for an entry-level correctional officer slot. However, his work record was spotty, and the reason for his departure from the police department was unclear. Although no one would talk openly about it, rumors were circulating that there had been allegations of police brutality against him. Since you do not want an unqualified and questionable political hack in your organization, you shelved his application.

After a week Senator Nester's office called "on behalf of a constituent" and inquired about the son-in-law's application. Your personnel officer told the senator's office that a letter had been sent to the applicant thanking him for his application but informing him that applications were competitive and, unfortunately, he had not been selected. Later in the day, an enraged Senator Nester called back in person. "Why wasn't I informed of the turn down? I've done a hell of a lot for this correctional system and have a right to expect the courtesy of a reply. I never had this problem before." His next statement was a clear threat. "You may find that these upcoming hearings will question your practices in dealing with the legislature, and I'll have some questions about your personnel policies, too." When you had a chance to speak, you told Senator Nester that you were running the institution, and until you were replaced you would continue to hire people based on merit.

Two months later at budget hearings in the legislature, you found out Senator Nester was a man of his word. Because of his influence, a new car for the prison superintendent was stricken, slots for 18 new correctional officers were also stricken, and to make matters worse, the committee voted to nullify the badly needed pay raises that had been budgeted for all the prison employees.

The senator's message has come through to you "loud and clear." You realize that the two of you will have to reach some sort of working agreement, unless you can marshal enough support from friendlier legislators, which does not seem likely. The question for you now is how to approach Senator Nester. How can you maintain your standards and at the same time appease him? Should you give and take a little, should you look for a new job, or should you do both? You are not a quitter; you would prefer to work with Senator Nester, but you keep asking yourself how.

Questions for Discussion

In this particular case, it appears that you, the superintendent, must initiate a reconciliation with the senator. Was the rift that developed between the two of you completely necessary? If you had done your homework and learned how powerful the senator was, would you have handled the situation more discreetly? What could you have done differently, and what can you do now?

Case 3

Prison Sexuality

You have been superintendent of the state adult correctional facility for six months. Having worked in the field of corrections for over ten years, you have developed quite a list of improvements you would like to implement. These changes include a number of areas in security and treatment.

You can remember when you started out your correctional career as a security officer. After six years of service you were promoted to a security supervisor. Years later you transferred into the counseling department at level III. Your transfer coincided with your graduation from a nearby university, which you had been attending part-time for a number of years. With your newly earned master's degree in correctional counseling, you attempted to strengthen your institution's treatment program, particularly in the area of crisis intervention, and had achieved some degree of success. In your most recent position, you served successfully as an assistant superintendent at a smaller medium-security institution.

Currently, as superintendent, you have methodically worked through your list of improvements. It is six months later, and you have come to item number four: How to deal effectively with the problems of prison sexuality, particularly sexual assault and the rapidly escalating HIV problem.

Sexual assaults by aggressive older male inmates against younger prisoners have continued to increase at the prison. It is one thing to tolerate homosexual relationships between consenting adults but quite another to deal with the young and sometimes older victims of homosexual rape. Of all the difficult situations in which you have found yourself as a prison administrator, the most difficult by far have been the sessions with rape victims. Depressed, humiliated, and emotionally torn apart, they looked to you as a correctional administrator for help, and usually there was little solace you could give them. Sure, you could transfer them to another prison or place them in administrative segregation, but that would provide only a partial solution. You could never guarantee them that they would not be attacked again. They knew what the situation was and, as a result, usually refused to identify their assailants out of fear of an even worse attack as retaliation.

There are a number of theories concerning the best way to handle sexual problems in prison. A well-respected colleague of yours isolated all prisoners with a history of sexual violence in a single cell block. Another superintendent housed all suspected aggressive homosexuals in a special prison camp, and other administrators tried to segregate all potential rape victims from the general inmate population. Each of these approaches has positive and negative qualities, and you are not sure which one is best. Your institution, which was built in the late 1930s, averages between 40 and 50 serious sexual assaults each year that are reported or confirmed by correctional officers. Of course, there is no way to know how many assaults actually occur, since many go unreported. Further, none of these options protect against correctional staff, which far too often become intimately involved with inmates. You are not sure which approach would be most effective, but as prison superintendent you intend to take the lead in developing a strategy to deal with sexual problems in your prison.

As if sexual assaults weren't enough, there is also the sexually transmitted disease problem. Out of a population of approximately 1,500 adult male inmates, 85 have tested positive for HIV and another 110 have other forms of STDs. The prison staff is generally somewhat ill at ease regarding the inmates who are known to have sexually transmitted diseases. In fact, four employees have resigned because of their apprehension. Of course the inmates who have similar feelings have no such choice. In fact, you admit to yourself that you personally share their feelings of uneasiness and concern. Although HIV research has come a long way toward finding effective treatment, these expensive drugs are not readily available inside the prison. Further, you want to make sure to maintain strict confidentiality so that inmates with HIV do not become targets of prison violence.

You want to make a serious and sustained attempt to effectively address the sexual problems in your prison, but you feel somewhat overwhelmed, especially with the problem of sexually transmitted diseases. Still, you are determined to try.

Questions for Discussion

In this particular case, would a conjugal or furlough program be more feasible? What might be some of the advantages and disadvantages of each? What are some ways in which you can include security staff members in a comprehensive rape-prevention and treatment program? What about STD education, including outside organizations to provide information and services?

Case 4

Progressive Administration, Punitive Community

MEMO

TO: Assistant Superintendent, Joan White

FROM: Superintendent Ralph Harris

RE: Complaints of Concerned Citizens Committee

Please forward to me, within 48 hours of your meeting on June 6th with the committee, your assessment of their concerns and plan for addressing them. Needless to say, we don't want this thing to snowball.

June 6th was yesterday, the report to the superintendent is due tomorrow, and you still aren't sure what to recommend. The Concerned Citizens Committee, or CCC as they like to refer to themselves, is a group of about 100 men and women who want action regarding the imprisonment and punishment of people they refer to as "dangerous individuals." The committee has grown by about 25 members a week since an escape occurred four weeks ago when a local farmer's truck was stolen. The escapee was captured within 5 days and the truck was returned to the owner, undamaged. Still, fear and panic had been the response of this small rural community of 3,000 people. They over-looked the economic advantages of the new 1,000-bed facility located in their economically depressed county and instead focused on, as they put it in the meeting, "the killers and rapists wasting taxpayers' dollars in an air-conditioned country club." None of the committee had actually visited the new prison, although one person claimed she had a cousin who was fired after 2 weeks on the job because he wouldn't cater to the wishes of the inmates.

The meeting had been very emotional, and you had to bear the brunt of their anxiety and anger concerning what they imagined rather than knew about the running of the prison and its occupants. You had to listen patiently to such expressions as: "Why are you giving convicts a free education when I have to pay for my children's college?"; "If you ask me, you ought to execute the whole bunch of them and save everybody a lot of trouble"; and "We are going to get the governor to close that place down before somebody gets out of there and rapes or kills our wives and children."

Your being a female corrections administrator didn't help matters any. You couldn't help but notice the disapproving looks of the women who attended the meeting. In fact, you overheard one of them comment to a friend, "Why didn't she choose to be a teacher or a nurse? Working in a prison is no place for a lady." As if that weren't bad enough, when you left the meeting, a middle-aged man said to you with a sly grin on his face, "So you like to be around dangerous men?" You didn't respond to him, but if looks could kill. . . . A follow-up meeting had been scheduled in 2 weeks, and now you are faced with presenting a report and recommendations to Superintendent Harris. The situation seems pretty hopeless, but something has to be done. Public relations are important, but sometimes public ignorance and fear is hard to overcome. This situation is proving to be a big test for you personally and professionally. You hope you can pass it.

Questions for Discussion

What do you think are some reasons why members of the community feel the way they do about the prison? What kinds of factors contribute to the development of such attitudes? What can you do to address the negative attitudes of the committee? As a female corrections administrator, how does your being a woman influence the concerned citizens? Are there ways you can use the fact that you are a woman to your advantage?

Case 5

Too Little Supervision or an Unfortunate Incident?

The county jail can accommodate prisoners in a large holding cell called the "Bull Pen." There are also eight other cells designed to accommodate two persons each. Women and juveniles are taken to the next county to a regional jail serving the surrounding four counties. On Saturday nights the jail is usually full with the same repeat drunks and hell-raisers. In addition, there are usually one or two dangerous felons awaiting transport to the state penitentiary, two or three indicted for felonies awaiting trial for offenses ranging from murder to fraud, some misdemeanants who are serving out their time, and one or two pretrial detainees who cannot make bail.

Three deputies are assigned to oversee the jail, two during the day, and one at night. The one working the night shift also helps the dispatcher with intake processing and handles the radio in the dispatcher's absence. The facility is about 25 years old and takes on the characteristics of a "zoo" when it is full. Nevertheless, it is solid and well built, and there has never been a breakout. The population averages about 21, day in and day out. You, as the chief county correctional officer, are usually on the day shift. You stay busy with booking, inventory, release, court appearances, overseeing visits, mail delivery, and phone calls. When one of your correctional officers is sick or on vacation, a deputy from the patrol division may be called in by the sheriff to help as needed. This Sunday you are working the graveyard shift for an officer who is taking some vacation time.

A deputy from the patrol division brought in a 20-year-old male, who attended a local university, for drunk driving. The young man, obviously drunk and sick, was found in his car on the side of the road near the state park where a rock band had been in concert that day. James Bright was from a nearby town and had no previous record. He was melancholy, contrite, and drunk. It was 2:00 AM when you locked Bright up in a vacant cell after taking his personal property. There is a clear view down the aisle from the desk at the reception counter where the officer in charge can see and hear what is going on. You can shut the steel door to the aisle if necessary, but usually it is open in compliance with jail operating procedure. The jail operating procedure also specified: "periodic cell checks at irregular intervals, but not less than one an hour apart."

Aside from some snoring and moaning, the jail cells seemed quiet. You checked all the offense reports and determined who will be getting out in the morning. The sheriff wanted them out before breakfast, if possible, so he can save on meal costs. You made a couple of phone calls and the radio started popping. The highway patrol had a driver's license checkpoint in the next county, and some motorists were turning off just before the checkpoint and heading for a bypass route in your county. The radio operator turned rather pale. It seemed his wife was caught at the checkpoint with someone in the car when she was supposed to be home. The operator asked you to handle dispatch for an hour while he checked out the situation with his wife. He left before you had a chance to respond to his request. The night passed, and the radio operator eventually returned in a foul mood.

It was 6:00 AM when you took a walk down the aisle and started calling the names of people to be released. You called for James Bright but no one answered. You called again; no answer. When you got to Bright's cell to awaken him, he appeared to have slipped off his bunk and seemed to be asleep on the floor. You opened the cell door and were shocked to see that Bright had made a noose from his shoelaces and tightened it around his neck. He had tied the other end to the bunk rail and laid down with the weight of his head and shoulders tightening the noose until he passed out. He had apparently died from strangulation. You called for the radio operator to summon the fire department's rescue truck while you untied the noose and began pounding on his chest. The cool body temperature indicated any efforts to revive were too late.

The sheriff viewed the scene and asked the dreaded question, "When did you check him last? Did you write it down in your log?"

"Sheriff," you respond. "I checked all of them two or three times after I booked him in at 2:00 AM; he looked all right to me. I did have to watch the radio for an hour or two while Jimmy got his wife from the highway patrol road block. There wasn't a sound coming from that cell that would make me the least bit suspicious."

The sheriff looked around the jail. The rest of the prisoners were restless, hanging on the cell bars. One shouted, "Sheriff, I want out of here! It ain't safe here. Somebody must have killed that kid. You know you can't hang yourself off no bed!"

"Shut up," responded the sheriff. He was beginning to see a potential problem.

After the coroner had finished his fact gathering and estimating the time of death, it was apparent that you had missed one, maybe two checks. Although you had recorded all the checks on the log, the neat row of checks and times looked like they were all recorded at the same time, a not-unheard-of practice by custodial personnel at the end of the night shift. The good news, if there was any, was that the death was probably a suicide.

The family complained, and the FBI came to investigate. You were censured for untying the ligature rather than cutting it, and for falsifying the log of cell checks. This fact was easily developed from interviewing prisoners in the adjacent cells.

It was not 100% proven that Bright was not murdered, but the preponderance of evidence pointed to suicide. The lawsuit asked for unspecified damages and alleged that the sheriff failed to properly train his jail staff, failed to provide proper supervision of the jail when the radio operator was out, and failed to provide a safe environment for his prisoners. Particularly, the suit alleged that the correctional officers should have known Bright was a suicide risk. He was a white, 20-year-old male, a first offender and remorseful. Further, the failure of the correctional officer to remove Bright's long shoelaces was a negligent act indicative of the lack of training and supervision contributing materially to the absence of a safe environment in the jail.

After 6 months of legal expenses, the county's lawyers recommended a settlement offer of $300,000 with an initial offer of $150,000. The sheriff was told to do something to improve his jail operation. The sheriff was also asked to provide the county commissioners with a priority list of improvements to be made in the jail and cost estimates. The commissioners may have held the sheriff responsible for the jail's operation, but as the chief correctional officer, he held you responsible. Of course, after this, you might not be chief correctional officer for long. The sheriff passed the commissioners' request on to you with a curt reply that he wants the situation "cleaned up" by the end of the working day.

Questions for Discussion

Successful management at any level of corrections requires constant and diligent supervision. The courts have shown a willingness to hold state and local jurisdictions responsible for assuring constitutional standards in correctional facilities. What would be on your list of needs to improve supervision and safety within the jail and the training of operating personnel? What particular item would be your first priority and why? How about the chief correctional officer? What should be done about him?

Case 6

Managing a Women's Prison

You are the new superintendent at the state adult women's prison. No one believed you would continue working toward a career in correctional administration. Even your husband, a physician, from time to time doubted the value of your efforts. You persevered, and now, in your mid-30s and after 9 years of marriage, a career, and two children, you have been appointed superintendent.

After your first tour of the institution, you were somewhat disheartened. The drab green paint was peeling off the walls. The prison library consisted of 60 or so books and a ragged set of encyclopedias. The recreation room was poorly stocked with damaged equipment from the men's prison. The faces of the women pretty much reflected their environment and the winter season—depressed.

Your first objective was to remodel the facility—if painting the walls and repairing the heating system could be considered remodeling. In any event, two coats of paint and a new heating system later, the place at least looked more cheerful.

The administrative problems facing you are numerous and immense. The prison needs increased treatment, vocational, and educational programs; improved health care; additional facility renovations and additions; improvement in food preparation and quality; more effective prison security; and additional correctional personnel. Correcting the deficiencies in the women's prison would require not only sophisticated management skills but a substantially increased operating budget as well. The state commissioner's initial response to your budget request was not very supportive. Since women inmates comprise only 10% of the state's incarcerated adult offenders, the commissioner was reluctant to allocate funds he felt could be better utilized elsewhere.

You could not help feeling that his reluctance stems at least in part from his being a man; you feel that he does not give the women's prison the consideration it deserves because he is not aware of the needs of women. How could a man fully understand the special needs of female offenders? Somehow you have to help him become more aware of the female offender. Even if you can gain some budget increases, that probably will not be enough. Community resources may also be available if you can motivate local business and civic leaders. Being a female superintendent of a women's prison has proven to be as much of a challenge as you thought it would. Changes need to be made. You have the will and now must find the way.

Questions for Discussion

What are some ways that you, as the new superintendent of the women's prison, could encourage support for needed changes? Perhaps the state commissioner might be invited to visit the institution and talk to a group of female inmates. Could you write prominent women who are civic leaders and in state government and invite them to visit the prison and discuss issues and possible solutions?

Case 7

Where Do You Begin?

You accepted the governor's appointment to be commissioner of the Department of Corrections knowing that some very difficult decisions were looming regarding budget issues. You will also be confronting questions about the department's overall performance, since the governor made the Department of Corrections a very high-profile issue during his campaign.

Now the governor has met with you and has directed that $35 million be cut from the department's budget. You try to warn the governor that such a massive budget reduction will have catastrophic consequences for the department. The governor further instructs you to reorganize, downsize, and force as many senior, higher-paid staff to retire as possible. You must have a draft proposal to him within 30 days. As a matter of protocol, you feel obliged to inform the chairpersons of your House and Senate Corrections Committees of the pending budget cuts that you will soon be required to make. Both chairpersons are angered by the governor's directive to you, especially since he has not discussed it with them. There is going to be conflict between the governor and the legislature concerning the budget cuts, and you feel like you are caught in the middle.

No matter where you cut an already lean budget, morale will plummet among inmate and staff alike, making prison environments more unstable. Can technology in such areas as surveillance compensate for reductions in correctional officer staff positions? What about volunteer chaplains to cover the responsibilities of the two staff chaplains? Could food services absorb some of the budget reductions? You could ally yourself with House and Senate legislators, but if you lose, you might be fired. Or you could resign rather than be the "hatchet man" for the governor.

Questions for Discussion

You must examine every facet of your department's operations to determine where and how to most effectively achieve the necessary reductions. Where do you begin? How do you reassure the legislature and the citizenry that public safety will not be compromised by cuts to the Department of Corrections? Is such reassurance even possible? What action will you take?

SECTION VII

Correctional Ethics and Legal Issues

Ethics involves a wide range of discretionary decision making affected by philosophical, social, and political factors. The introduction to this section discusses a number of ethical and legal issues confronted by personnel within the correctional system. As you react to the seven cases, try to determine how your decisions are affected by your personal values and by the social and political environment—as well as the effect of those decisions on people around you.

Introduction

In recent years, ethics has been a primary topic in many venues. Frequently one hears of political decisions and ethics, governmental actions and ethics, or ethical considerations in everyday social events. Still, many people do not seem to know what the term means. Dictionaries define ethics as the discipline dealing with what is good and bad and with moral duty and obligation; and/or the principles of conduct governing an individual or group. One could define ethics as *the science of human duty*. When applied in a concrete moral context, doing one's duty could also mean doing what is right, regardless of the cost to oneself or others.

Ethics comprise the fundamental framework for how individuals conduct themselves within society. Individuals have personal ethical frameworks; at times, their ethical assessment of a given situation will differ from that of others. Issues such as abortion and capital punishment are controversial because what one person perceives as an unethical approach may seem perfectly appropriate to someone else. Ethics, morality and the law are related, but there are distinct differences. Members of society have a duty to both themselves and to other members to maintain social order and to protect the rights of all. Statutes and laws, as imperfect as they may be, prescribe rules for conduct. The law outlines the basic standards of behavior for society to function. Meeting legal obligations does not necessarily qualify as making ethical decisions.

Ethics within the realm of corrections can be very difficult to understand. Many of us feel that when someone breaks the law and is sentenced to a punishment, he or she gives up certain rights and privileges that exist within a free society. For example, individuals sentenced to probation often must agree to be subject to warrantless searches, along with restrictions on their movement and activities. Of course, those sentenced to serve time in a correctional facility are subject to much greater restrictions. In some instances, to some people, the forfeiture of these rights and privileges may seem extreme and uncalled for, even unethical. Still other persons may believe that legal sanctions should be even more severe.

Correctional Ethics

By its very nature, the field of corrections routinely involves situations in which one person has a substantial degree of power over another. Ethical misconduct occurs anytime a member of the correctional staff misuses their discretionary power for personal gain. This might include situations such as excessive force, sexual harassment, misappropriation of resources, smuggling contraband into a penal facility, etc. Regardless of the specific act involved, any form of misconduct threatens to undermine the legitimacy of the correctional system and can result in significant harm to the victim.

Correctional administrators must place ethics and integrity at the center of the organization and frequently discuss these issues with employees. Most agencies have professional codes of conduct, formal policies, and training that are designed to minimize unethical behavior. However, these policies are only as effective as their enforcement. Correctional agencies wishing to create an ethical workplace culture must develop mechanisms to detect and investigate misconduct, improve supervision of personnel, implement psychological testing in the hiring process, and promote employees based on merit instead of outside political influences (McCarthy & Perry-Bellmer, 2017). It is important to note that even the most vigilant employers will likely not be able to prevent or detect all ethical misconduct. The hope is that hiring quality employees and creating an ethics-based organizational culture will discourage misconduct and will promote the reporting of any misconduct that does occur.

Perhaps the first and most fundamental ethical decision in corrections belongs to the sentencing judge who must decide the proper punishment and/or treatment for each offender. This decision must balance the judge's personal ethics with his/her legal authority and the prevailing ethical principles of the community. Debates regarding how much discretion a judge should have in this process have been commonplace. The options available to judges declined with the rise of mandatory minimum sentencing laws.

The most common punishment is probation or a fine. While these punishments are typically far less punitive than incarceration, several ethical issues can arise. For example, probation fees appear to be increasing. Combined with restitution, fines, and other court costs, they can become insurmountable for the typical offender (Whitehead & Woodward, 2017). This could also lead to questions about the legitimacy or fairness of sentencing and whether the sentence is meant to benefit society or simply to produce revenue.

Another ethical issue involves the risk-assessment tools that are used to determine, among other things, whether incarceration is appropriate and the level of supervision that is required within a community or institutional corrections setting. These decisions have profound impacts on the offender's experience within the justice system and the ability to reintegrate into society. Some scholars argue that many of the risk factors included on these tests (e.g., criminal peer association, marital status, socioeconomic status, criminal history) have disproportionately punitive impacts on marginalized groups (Harcourt, 2015; Starr, 2015). Even if these tools are shown to accurately predict the offender's risk of engaging in future criminality, it could be argued that this is a form of systemic discrimination.

Evolution of Prisoners' Rights

People sentenced to incarceration receive the most punitive restrictions on the liberties granted in the Constitution. It should be no surprise, then, that most lawsuits challenging correctional policies affect inmates in penal institutions. There was a long tradition known as the *hands-off doctrine* under which courts feared that they would violate the separation of powers if they intervened in the operation of state penal institutions. The courts also believed they did not have the expertise to decide prison management issues.

The civil rights movement, increased public concern about prisoner welfare, and a number of prison riots combined to spur a new judicial philosophy beginning in the 1960s (Mushlin & Galt, 2009). The Civil Rights Act of 1871 §1983 was a long-standing mechanism for seeking redress for deprivation of federal constitutional and statutory rights by persons acting under color of state law (behavior of state or local government staff during employment). *Monroe v. Pape* (1961) established that state employees can be sued under §1983 for deprivation of legal rights. Only a few federal statutes apply to prisoners (Americans with Disabilities Act and the Religious Land Use and Institutionalized Persons Act are the primary statutes plus the Religious Freedom Reformation Act for federal prisoners). The most important Supreme Court decisions have centered on four constitutional rights: First Amendment rights of free speech and religious practice; Fourth Amendment rights pertaining to unreasonable searches and seizures; Eighth Amendment rights concerning cruel and unusual punishment, and Fourteenth Amendment rights to due process and equal treatment (Shelden, Brown, Miller & Fritzler, 2016).

Cooper v. Pate (1964) was a landmark case that ended the judicial hands-off doctrine and verified that prisoners were entitled to protection under §1983 to challenge the conditions of their confinement in the courts. Black Muslim inmates at a prison in Illinois were not allowed to congregate, to observe diet or clothing requirements of their religion, or to purchase religious publications—privileges accorded other inmates. The Supreme Court ruled all state prisoners have equal rights to practice their religious beliefs. In *Wolff v. McDonnell* (1974), the Supreme Court ruled that inmates have not lost all privileges—"there is no iron curtain drawn between the Constitution and the prisons of this country." The decision established some due process rights for prisoners in disciplinary hearings. Courts recognized and affirmed the civil rights of prisoners regarding freedom of religion, safety, medical care, housing, mail, and the rights of juveniles.

In response to perceived frivolous prisoner litigation in the federal courts Congress passed the Prison Litigation Reform Act (PLRA) in 1996. The Act places restrictions on lawsuits by prisoners that do not apply to other people filing lawsuits. The restrictions apply to anyone who is incarcerated, including pretrial detainees who have not been tried and are presumed innocent under the law. PLRA requires inmates to exhaust all administrative remedies at the confining institution—taking complaints through all levels of the grievance system at a prison, jail, or juvenile institution—prior to filing lawsuits. Prisoners cannot seek redress for mental or emotional injuries alone (Shelden et al., 2016). PLRA restricts the power of the courts to remedy conditions, requiring that the needs, capacities, and budgets of the institutions be taken into consideration. It also limits the amount paid to attorneys.

Ronald Nussle filed a suit charging that correction officers had singled him out for a severe beating. He did not first file his grievance with the Connecticut Department of Correction. As a result, the district court dismissed his suit for failure to follow PLRA requirements. The Court of Appeals reversed, saying administrative remedies need not be exhausted for single incidents that affect only particular prisoners. In *Porter v. Nussle* (2002), the Supreme Court unanimously decided that the exhaustion requirements of PLRA apply to all inmate suits about prison life. However, in *Jones v. Bock* (2007), the court ruled that failure to exhaust administrative remedies for one claim does not require dismissal of the entire claim and that the burden of proving exhaustion of all administrative remedies does not fall on the plaintiff.

Prisoner rights have declined steadily in the last several decades (Mushlin & Galtz, 2009). The legal gains of the 1970s have been replaced with judicial decisions that grant corrections officials latitude in their efforts to manage a prison—essentially allowing the constitutional rights of prisoners to be compromised because of the difficulties of running a prison. For example, one common violation of prisoner rights is administrative segregation. Prison officials can place an inmate in solitary confinement for protection from her/himself or from others. The determination of the need for protection, however, is open to abuse (Shelden et al., 2016). Some have suggested that the current era could be characterized as *hands semi-off*.

Issues such as overcrowding of custodial facilities are complex, complicated by strained budgets and public attitudes. The courts must balance safeguarding the civil rights of convicts with the ability of local government and prison authorities to maintain security, safety, and discipline within the prisons. Ethical considerations encompass almost every facet of prison life and administration. Whenever the Supreme Court hands down decisions regarding prisoners' rights, they satisfy some constituents and enrage others. Still, their decisions continue to attempt to maintain a viable balance between the rights of the kept with the duties and needs of the keepers.

Overcrowding

Overcrowding is a problem in corrections because at some point it becomes a violation of the prisoner's Eighth Amendment rights. The problem intensified during the period of mass incarceration when prison was deemed the appropriate punishment for an increasing number of criminal offenses. Overcrowding is accompanied by ethical problems such as prisoner victimization by other prisoners and unlawful conduct by custodial officers, including brutality, extortion, and graft. It creates a feeling of frustration and helplessness throughout the staff, robbing them of the energy and motivation to bring about creative changes. It is no wonder that overcrowding is recognized as the most pressing problem in corrections today.

Overcrowding is not just an issue of numbers of inmates and space available. For example, double bunking two persons in a one-person cell may not be unconstitutional in and of itself (*Rhodes v. Chapman*, 1981), but double bunking two in a cell when the cell mates are from rival gangs is unconstitutional (*Walsh v. Mellas*, 1988). Overcrowding becomes a constitutional issue when it inflicts wanton or unnecessary pain or is excessive to the severity of the crime committed (*Coker v. Georgia*, 1977). Given this standard, it would appear that jails would be the most vulnerable to constitutional issues arising from overcrowding because they house mostly pretrial detainees and misdemeanants. A higher standard of care is thus required because of the lesser severity of the crime committed—or, in the case of pretrial detainees, perhaps no crime at all.

While 16.5% of jails operated at more than 100% capacity, the average daily jail population declined from its peak of 95% in 2007 to 80% in 2016 (Zeng, 2018). Even with the recent nationwide leveling out of the prison population, 14 states and the Federal Bureau of Prisons reported prison populations that exceeded capacity in 2016 (Carson, 2018). Often, the only options available to the state are to expand and build, to contract with the private sector or with county jails, to develop new community programs, or to revise parole eligibility.

For decades courts intervened to force states to reduce crowding in their facilities, to maintain humane conditions in prisons, to discipline violent correctional staff, and to provide basic health care (Burkhardt & Jones, 2016). Court oversight continued until the states or cities could demonstrate that they had made the required improvements. In some cases, the supervision lasted decades. In 2011, the Supreme Court in *Brown v. Plata* (see table 1) ruled that California's overcrowded prison system was unconstitutional. The prison system was ordered to reduce the overcrowding from almost 200% to 137.5% of capacity. Although limited to California, Jonathan Simon (2014) believes the case is significant for its reflection of cultural attitudes that there are limits to the abuse and mistreatment of prisoners. The conditions created by mass incarceration made the punishment cruel and unusual, and the court took the unprecedented action of ordering California to reduce its prison population by 40,000.

> *Brown v. Plata* has revealed that prisons hold many people who are not a danger to anyone, perhaps never were, and could certainly be managed with less danger to themselves and no additional danger to others through alternatives to prison. Many of these prisoners are burdened with multiple chronic illnesses, including mental illness, which is irreversibly worsened by incarceration. (p. 159)

Elimination of unlawful overcrowding and other unconstitutional conditions will not be solved in the long run by prisoner lawsuits, or by

Table 1   Prisoners' Rights

First Amendment Mail Rights

Procunier v. Martinez (1974) found that the practice of reading and censoring outgoing and incoming correspondence from and to prisoners was unconstitutional unless the practices were essential to legitimate penological objectives of the correctional system.

Turner v. Safley (1987) ruled that there was a legitimate penological interest in forbidding correspondence between inmates in different institutions, namely the prohibition of communicating escape plans and/or assaults.

Thornburgh v. Abbott (1989) held that incoming mail may be rejected if it is found to be a detriment to the security, good order, or discipline of the institution, or if it could facilitate criminal activity.

Beard v. Banks (2006) extended the *Thornburgh* ruling, holding that Pennsylvania's justification of withholding newspapers, magazines, and personal photographs from inmates in the long-term segregation unit to improve behavior was a legitimate government purpose.

First Amendment Religious Rights

Cruz v. Beto (1971) declared that inmates may exercise their religious beliefs as long as the practices of a particular faith do not violate prison regulations.

O'lone v. Estate of Shabazz (1987) ruled that restrictions on the free exercise of religion plausibly advanced the goals of security in the institution.

Cutter v. Wilkinson (2005) rejected Ohio's challenge to the Religious Land Use and Institutionalized Persons Act (RLUIPA) as violating the Establishment Clause of the First Amendment. (The Act, passed in 2000, prohibited establishing a substantial burden on prisoners in exercising their religion unless the burden furthered a compelling government interest.)

Holt v. Hobbs (2015) allowed an inmate to grow a beard in accordance with his religious beliefs because the prison failed to show how their prohibition presented a security risk.

First Amendment Visitation Rights

Newman v. Alabama (1977) held that inmates have a right to visitation privileges on a regular basis.

Block v. Rutherford (1984) ruled that contact visits can jeopardize the security of the facility. (Jail inmates had challenged the jail's policy of allowing only noncontact visits by pretrial detainees with their spouses, relatives, and friends.)

Kentucky Department of Corrections v. Thompson (1989) found that Kentucky prison regulations that excluded visits from particular individuals without a hearing did not create a protected liberty interest in visitation privileges. The denial of prison access was based on reasonable grounds to believe the presence of certain visitors could interfere with the orderly operation of the institution.

Overton v. Bazzetta (2003) rejected the challenge of Michigan inmates to restrictions on visitation rights. The court found some liberties and privileges enjoyed by other citizens are surrendered by incarceration; freedom of association is one of the rights least compatible with incarceration.

Fourth Amendment Privacy Rights

Bell v. Wolfish 1979) established that cavity searches of pretrial detainees did not violate individual liberty, due process, or privacy rights as long as the practices were implemented in the interest of security.

(continued)

Hudson v. Palmer (1984) held that an inmate does not have a right to privacy in a prison cell because of the institution's paramount interest in security, but a prisoner's personal property is protected from intentional destruction at the hands of prison officials.

Eighth Amendment Medical Rights

Estelle v. Gamble (1976) affirmed that medical and health care were constitutional rights of prisoners.

Washington v. Harper (1990) held that an inmate could be administered psychiatric drugs if dangerous to himself or others.

Helling v. McKinney (1993) supported an inmate who asserted that his health was endangered by sharing a cell with a man who smoked five cigarettes a day. The court ruled that if McKinney could prove his health claims and that prison officials acted with indifference, he would be entitled to relief.

Pennsylvania Department of Corrections v. Yeskey (1998) ruled unanimously that the protections of the Americans with Disabilities Act extended to prisoners and that there could be no discrimination based on disability. (An inmate had been denied participation in a boot-camp program that could have resulted in early parole after administrators discovered his history of hypertension.)

Brown v. Plata (2011) ordered California to reduce overcrowding in its prisons because of its failure to provide adequate medical attention, thus reinforcing the duty of correctional facilities to provide health care.

Eighth Amendment Overcrowding

Hutto v. Finney (1978) found that the overcrowded, filthy conditions in the prisons in Arkansas plus inadequate food combined with punitive isolation for more than thirty days constituted cruel and unusual punishment.

Rhodes v. Chapman (1982) held that overcrowding *per se* is not necessarily a condition that violates the Eighth Amendment. To be cruel and unusual there must be wanton and unnecessary infliction of pain or conditions grossly disproportionate to the severity of the crime warranting punishment.

Whitley v. Albers (1986) ruled that prison officials can use excessive force to subdue a disturbance; the force is unconstitutional only if used maliciously.

Wilson v. Seiter (1991) required that in addition to demonstrating inhumane conditions, a plaintiff must prove that corrections officers were deliberately indifferent to the suffering caused—the intentions and capabilities of officials became the standard rather than brutal conditions.

Hudson v. McMillian (1992) found that excessive physical force against a prisoner may constitute cruel and unusual punishment even without a demonstration of a significant injury.

Farmer v. Brennan (1994) held that prison officials' deliberate indifference to the substantial risk of serious harm to a transsexual inmate confined in the general population constituted cruel and unusual punishment. (The Prison Rape Elimination Act was passed nine years later and cited this case.)

Brown v. Plata (2011) required California to reduce its prison population due to unconstitutional conditions created by overcrowding.

Millbrook v. United States (2013) established that inmates sexually assaulted by correctional officers can sue under the Federal Torts Claims Act. Prior to *Millbrook*, relief from sexual assault was limited to constitutional claims, which require a higher burden of proof.

Fourteenth Amendment Due Process Rights

Johnson v. Avery (1969) found that an inmate has the right to receive legal aid from another prisoner.

Morrisey v. Brewer (1972) ruled that Iowa must conduct an evidentiary hearing to determine probable cause prior to revoking parole.

Gagnon v. Scarpelli (1973) extended the requirement for revocation hearings to probationers. The court said the state, although not constitutionally obliged to provide counsel at the hearings, should do so for indigent probationers/parolees or in cases involving complicated documentary evidence.

Procunier v. Martinez (1974) held that inmates are entitled to file their grievances with the court.

Wolff v. McDonnell (1974) declared that while prisoners are not entitled to full due process protections, disciplinary proceedings must include written notice to the defendant of the charges, a written statement of evidence, and the opportunity for an inmate to call witnesses and present evidence.

Baxter v. Palmigiano (1976) ruled that inmates do not have the right to counsel in disciplinary hearings.

Bounds v. Smith (1976) found that inmates must have access to law libraries when there is an absence of adequate direct legal assistance.

Meachem v. Fano (1976) ruled that decisions to transfer inmates from one institution to another are not subject to judicial process under due process rights.

Hewitt v. Helms (1983) held that prison staff must provide minimal due process procedures before placing an inmate in restrictive confinement.

Superintendent v. Hill (1985) ruled that procedural due process requires only that prison disciplinary boards have some evidence in the record that supports their findings.

Murray v. Giarratano (1989), in a case involving indigent Virginia death row inmates, found that neither the Eighth amendment nor the Due Process Clause required states to provide counsel for post-conviction proceedings.

Sandin v. Conner (1995) held that there was no due process violation when an inmate was confined in isolation for two months for a disciplinary infraction without a hearing to substantiate the charge.

Lewis v. Smith (1996) ruled there was no violation of the law library requirements in *Bounds* after inmates alleged Arizona officials provided inadequate legal research facilities. The court said the prior ruling did not guarantee inmates access to material to transform themselves into "litigating engines."

Shaw v. Murphy (2001) held that inmates do not have a First Amendment right to provide legal assistance to other inmates.

Fourteenth Amendment Equal Treatment Rights

Lee v. Washington (1968) affirmed the unconstitutionality of state statutes requiring segregated prisons and jails.

Johnson v. California (2005) declared that California's policy of racial segregation in prison housing assignments must further a compelling governmental interest. All classifications using race should be viewed with strict scrutiny and narrowly tailored to achieve a compelling objective.

the federal government taking over state correctional systems. It will instead be solved in a change in the way in which the community views their correctional problems. Just as the community has come to recognize the need for dedicated public school teachers and new school facilities, a new community standard must evolve in which the community more carefully matches the punishment with the crime and is willing to accept the financial responsibility to carry it out in a way that extends the American civil rights tradition to those incarcerated.

Privatization of Correctional Facilities

Recently the issue of privatizing certain elements of corrections has been subject to intense debate. Corrections programs in many states have turned to private organizations to serve several correctional functions. For example, private companies often provide probation services, drug and alcohol treatment, and various operational functions (e.g., food service and health care) to correctional institutions. Most research has centered on private companies that own and operate entire prisons (Lindsey, Mears, & Cochran, 2016). However, the ethical issues surrounding privatization apply equally to any contracting of government functions to private entities.

In 2016, there were 94,164 state prisoners and 34,159 federal prisoners housed in privately-operated institutions—9% of all state and federal inmates (Carson, 2018). States vary significantly in their use of private facilities—22 states do not contract with private facilities; New Mexico houses 43% of its incarcerated population in private facilities, Montana 39%, Oklahoma 27%, Tennessee 26%, and Hawaii 25%. The number of people housed in private prisons increased 45% since 2000 (Sentencing Project, 2017).

For many persons, this poses an ethical dilemma—should profit-oriented organizations be supervising and treating convicted criminals? Proponents argue that private businesses run more efficiently and economically than bureaucratic state and local facilities. Critics of privatization argue that the quality of supervision and programs might suffer as a result of the cost-saving measures. Recent research suggests that privately-operated facilities do not provide a significant cost savings (Lundahl, Kunz, Brownell, Harris, & Vleet, 2009). Some research has found that private prisons are comparable to public facilities in terms of quality (Burkhardt & Jones, 2016; Makarios & Maahs, 2012) and inmate outcomes (Duwe & Clark, 2013; Powers, Kaukinen, & Jeanis, 2017).

The Department of Justice (DOJ) announced in 2016 that it would no longer use private prisons to house federal inmates because they did not maintain the same level of safety and security, did not save substantially on costs, and did not provide the same level of correctional services, programs, and resources as did government facilities (Zapotosky, 2017). The new administration reversed that decision. In 2017, there were 21,366 federal inmates in 12 privately run facilities.

One major ethical concern is that private companies have a financial interest in the continued growth of mass incarceration—more prisoners fuels their businesses. CoreCivic and the GEO Group contribute to political campaigns and lobby for punitive criminal justice policies that will increase reliance on prisons (Kappeler & Potter, 2018). Another ethical issue concerns the removal of prisoners from the state in which they were sentenced, placing emotional and financial burdens on families and inmates. The social consequences of exporting prisoners are enormous.

The Ultimate Punishment: Death

Probably the most difficult of the ethical controversies that exist in corrections is capital punishment. The Supreme Court ruled in *Furman v. Georgia* (1972) that existing death penalty statutes were implemented in an arbitrary and capricious manner with great potential for racial discrimination. States revised their death penalty statutes to overcome the court's objections. The revised Georgia system was approved in *Gregg v. Georgia* (1976). The primary revision was the required presentation of aggravating and mitigating evidence.

From 1976 to May 2018, there have been 1,474 executions (Death Penalty Information Center, 2018). Executions in the United States peaked in 1999 when 98 inmates were executed; in 2017 there were 23 executions. In July 2017, there were 2,817 inmates awaiting execution, many in states who have executed less than five inmates since 1976. Most inmates sentenced to death will die of natural causes well before they are executed. The United Nations has listed the death penalty as a human rights violation (Gehrke, 2017). The death penalty is now outlawed in England, most of Europe, and most of the English-speaking Western world, except the United States (Amnesty International, 2017). In the United States, 19 states and the District of Columbia have banned the death penalty (Fins, 2017). Both internationally and domestically, the trend is toward the abolition of the death penalty. Through the 1970s, belief that executions deter murder was a primary rationale for the death penalty. That justification declined significantly for scholars, policy makers, the general public, and law enforcement personnel (Radelet & Lacock, 2008). In a survey, 80% of leading criminologists concluded that empirical research demonstrated that the death penalty was not more effective a deterrent than long-term imprisonment. Researchers continue to study and debate the deterrent effect of the death penalty (Whitehead, Dodson, & Edwards, 2013).

Research on the death penalty in the post-*Furman* era indicates that the new statutes have not eliminated racial and other biases (Kappeler & Potter, 2018). "Racial discrimination has been the single most troubling issue for the death penalty in the United States in the past fifty years. It never goes away" (Gross, 2012, p. 1907). The Supreme Court, however, has "almost never found systemic racial discrimination in the administration of criminal justice by the states" (p. 1909). *McCleskey v. Kemp* (1987) is one of the most controversial decisions in the history of the Supreme Court. The majority argued that McCleskey had not proven racial bias by anyone involved in his case; broad patterns of racial discrimination were not proof of constitutional violations. The defendant needed to prove both that a decision maker acted with intentional discrimination **and** that the behavior affected the outcome.

Cases involving a minority defendant and a white victim are more likely to be tried as capital cases and are more likely to result in death sentences. Since 1976, over 78% of murder victims in cases resulting in an execution were white (Death Penalty Information Center, 2018). There have been 305 black defendants executed for cases in which the victims were white; 34 white defendants were executed for cases in which the victims were black. Of all post-*Furman* executions, 34.3% have been of African Americans.

The region of the country in which the defendant is prosecuted significantly impacts death-sentencing decisions (Kappeler & Potter, 2018). More people (122) have been tried, convicted, and executed by Harris County (TX, which includes the city of Houston), since 1976 than by any state other than Texas itself. Class also affects capital cases; the criminal justice system deals almost exclusively with poor people. Law professor Stephen Bright (2015) advises that the most fundamental element of fairness in an adversarial system of justice is representation by competent counsel. The remarkably poor quality legal representation in some capital cases is accompanied by "the even more remarkable indifference of courts" (p. 686).

Justice Stephen Breyer's dissent to *Sireci v. Florida* (2016) included this opinion.

> Individuals who are executed are not the "worst of the worst" but, rather, are individuals chosen at random on the basis, perhaps of geography, perhaps of the views of individual prosecutors, or still worse on the basis of race. . . . The time has come for this court to reconsider the constitutionality of the death penalty.

Policy makers are increasingly concerned about the costs associated with the death penalty (Aviram & Newby, 2013). Some states spend millions of dollars each year to operate a death row system that in many cases rarely carries out executions. California last executed an inmate in 2005. Since 1978, it has spent more than $4 billion on trials, automatic appeals, habeas corpus petitions and appeals, and the costs of incarceration on death row (Death Penalty Information Center, 2018). Capital cases in Oklahoma cost more than three times as much as non-capital cases. Florida spends $51 million more annually than it would cost to punish all first-degree murderers with life in prison without parole.

The possibility of someone innocent being put to death is a major ethical concern about the death penalty. The public and politicians often paid little attention to the possible innocence of people convicted of capital crimes until the last half of the 1990s. In 1996, Illinois exonerated five death row inmates. From 1988 to 2004, 14 people sentenced to die in Illinois were released from death row because of serious questions about their guilt. In 2000, former Governor George Ryan declared a moratorium on executions until the issue could be studied. Illinois abolished capital punishment in 2011. Wrongful convictions occur in homicide trials, and innocent people receive death sentences (Bohm, 2017). Since 1973, 162 people have been released from death row in 27 states due to actual or probable innocence (DPIC, 2018). Supporters of the death penalty may find this an acceptable risk because the chance of wrongful conviction is so small, but one must take into account that when such a mistake occurs it cannot be reversed.

Since 1976, executions have been carried out using a gas chamber (11), firing squad (3), hanging (3), and electrocution (158); the most common method of execution is lethal injection (1,299) (Death Penalty Information Center, 2018). Corrections officials and policy makers view lethal injection as the most humane form of execution. It is certainly easier on the witnesses and less expensive to administer. In reality, there is no absolute humane form of putting one's fellow man to death, a fact that must have crossed the mind of the families of victims many times.

Lethal injection is a profoundly flawed method for executions (Marceau & Chen, 2014). Death penalty states and the federal government used a three-drug sequence developed by Oklahoma in 1977 until forced to seek new combinations. The three drugs were sodium thiopental (a short-acting anesthetic); pancuronium bromide (muscle relaxant that paralyzes all voluntary muscles and causes suffocation); and potassium chloride (a toxin that induces cardiac arrest). People administering the drugs had little knowledge about their properties or what to do if the execution did not go as planned. Pancuronium created the appearance of a peaceful death, giving a false impression about the safety of the procedure. If the anesthetic did not work, the inmate would not convulse or exhibit signs of pain because movement was inhibited.

The Supreme Court ruled in *Baze v. Rees* (2008) that challenges to lethal injection procedures must show that the drug protocol poses a substantial risk of severe pain and that the state has refused to adopt a feasible alternative reducing that risk. Soon after *Baze*, death penalty states faced an unanticipated problem. The only U.S. supplier stopped making sodium thio-pental in August 2009. Plans to shift production to a facility in Italy failed when the Italian Parliament would only allow the drug to be used for medical purposes. Several states obtained supplies from a manufacturer in Great Britain until that country would not allow the drugs to be used for executions. Some states changed to a 1- or 2-drug protocol. Several states substituted pentobarbital or midazolam as the first drug. The results sometimes resulted in painful deaths that took almost two hours. Death penalty states have never been forthcoming about their procedures, but the lack of transparency has become even more pronounced with the shortage of drugs (Berger, 2014). Approximately half of the states do not allow external evaluation of their execution protocols. Secrecy acts shield suppliers and execution procedures from Freedom of Information Act requests.

In a challenge to Oklahoma's use of midazolam, the Supreme Court ruled in *Glossip v. Gross* (2015) that defendants had not proven that use of the drug was cruel and unusual and that they had not proposed an alternative method of execution. Justice Sonia Sotomayor dissented, arguing that scientific evidence has shown that midazolam is not sufficient to maintain unconsciousness until the other two drugs cause death. She also questioned the requirement of providing a reasonable alternative, arguing that a cruel method of execution does not become constitutional because of the lack of alternatives.

Arkansas had a supply of midazolam that expired April 30, 2017. Despite not having executed anyone since 2005, the state scheduled eight executions from April 17–27. After multiple legal challenges, four of the executions were stayed, and four individuals were executed within one week. Ford Vox (2016), a physician specializing in rehabilitation medicine, believes the United States is bumbling its way toward the end of the death penalty. As the number of executions decline, "the state-ordered deaths that we do commit become that much more unusual, freakish and unfair applications of the law. As states scramble to implement arbitrary new lethal injection protocols, the cruelty of the procedure only worsens."

Aside from the evidence related to whether the death penalty is an effective deterrent or is cost effective, the decision to support or reject the death penalty is ultimately an ethical one. Some people believe that taking a life maliciously or committing a heinous crime demonstrates a conscious and total disregard for society's rules and the lives of others, which warrants society's most severe penalty—death by execution. Others believe that life is protected by law and that it is inconsistent with the purpose of law for the government to take a life, no matter what the crime.

Summary

Corrections deals with multiple complex issues, and ethical concerns surface repeatedly when making decisions. One paramount consideration is that someone who commits a crime does not give up basic human rights. Discrimination, violence, overcrowding, correctional officer brutality, or withholding medial care cannot be overlooked just because they occur within the walls of a correctional facility or the offices of a probation department. Debate continues as to what rights are retained and what rights are forfeited because of the circumstances of incarceration.

Society often ignores the plight of those who have violated the law and feels that such problems do not concern them, but they do. Ethically, society's best interests are served by making sure that corrections is a viable part of society, not a separate entity.

Case 1

Offender Rights
and Public Expectations

You have been superintendent of the state prison for 5 years. Having to house, feed, and provide recreation and treatment for 2,000 inmates in a prison built for 1,200 has been difficult. In fact, you have begun to eat Rolaids like M&Ms. With the correctional officer's union threatening to strike, a stack of inmate lawsuits on your desk, and the typical problems of contraband and cell block assaults, all you need is another problem. Yet here it is. You glance once more at the letter from Reverend Hawkins:

Dear Superintendent Potter:

As a Christian brother, I entreat you to ban the subversive book circulating among the inmates by the self-proclaimed spiritual teacher who goes by the name of Yogi Bo. His book clearly encourages rebellion against the authority of the State and of God. Our chaplains have a difficult enough time reforming the unfortunate who find themselves in prison with the help of the Good Book. As difficult as it is, they are doing a remarkable job. To allow a book of other writings which challenge the God-given principles our country was founded on to circulate among the inmates will create an overwhelming burden to them and other God-fearing counselors, not to mention the risk of insurrection it poses to prison security.

The Ministerial Association is unanimously recommending that you ban this objectionable book.

We are praying that you will make the proper decision.

Sincerely,
Reverend Hawkins
President of the Ministerial Association

You shake your head, partly in frustration and partly in amusement, and take a deep breath. You were raised as a child in a Protestant church, and you and your wife have raised your children likewise. You share most of Reverend Hawkins's beliefs, but regardless of what you and the reverend believe, a great number of inmates don't feel or think the same way. Your prison is made up of Protestant Christians, Catholics, Native Americans, Black Muslims, two Hindus, one Buddhist, and a number of people who, if they believe in anything at all, probably believe in violence.

On the one hand, you have Reverend Hawkins and his supporters who want you to ban Yogi Bo's book. On the other hand, you have a relatively small yet vocal group of inmates who follow the teachings of Yogi Bo. You have read the book, and while you personally disagree with some of its ideas from your Christian viewpoint, you have found nothing advocating violence or rebellion. In fact, its message is basically a positive one and, to your surprise, you find yourself agreeing with a lot of the points Yogi Bo makes.

Popping another Rolaids in your mouth, you know you have got to make a decision. The easy thing to do would be to ban the book. Since the prison is located in a small rural area where Reverend Hawkins has substantial influence, such a decision would be good for you and the prison's image. If you don't ban the book, you will be criticized, letters will be written, and you might not even be reelected elder in the church you and your family attend. Still, you really believe that the inmates have the legal right to have the book, as it does not appear to be the threat that Reverend Hawkins and others think it is. In fact, you wonder if they have even read it. You reach for another Rolaids.

Questions for Discussion

Religious beliefs are very personal and powerful. There will be trouble, no matter which way you decide. What are some issues at stake here regarding the inmates' wishes and rights and the community's expectations? What role should your conscience play in your decision?

Case 2

A Choice of Punishments

You are an 18-year-old high school senior with nothing to do during the summer. No job, no summer school, no camps, nothing. For some reason, public summer programs for youth like you are very scarce or nonexistent. It is July 4th, hot, and you are looking for some diversion. Your friend, Paul Johnson, comes by in his antique pickup truck that he has spent the last 6 months rebuilding, and he invites you to a party that he will be attending at a friend's apartment in the projects. The friend's parents are away for the day. Although Paul is a few months older than you and dropped out of your high school, he always seems to have money, not much, but some. Paul tells you that he has to go by the grocery store and pick up a case of beer and also get some gas. You are impressed until Paul drives up to a two-pump Quick Stop, parks beside a car that is filling up so he cannot be seen by the cashier, fills up, then jumps in the truck and drives off. The attendant made the mistake of letting the pump run without being able to see the vehicle being filled up. You are not too happy with this, but it was so slick, the way he edged up to the pumps behind the other automobile, that there seems to be little danger of getting caught.

Next, Paul drives to a grocery store for beer; he parks at the corner of the building out of sight of the cashiers in the store and asks you to watch the truck because he wants to leave the motor running. "Sometimes it is hard to start when it is hot," explains Paul. You patiently wait and in a few minutes Paul comes out the doors of the grocery with a case of beer and drives off. Apparently, Paul legitimately purchased a case of beer and you are going to be able to share it with him at the party. "Good friend, old Paul," you mutter to yourself.

The next day your mother tells you there is a police officer at the door with a warrant for your arrest. Not only did the Quick Stop clerk get a description and partial license plate number, but the manager of the grocery store followed Paul out and got the full tag number as well

174

as a description of the occupants of the truck. Paul has already been arrested and identified you as his companion. In your state, accessories to misdemeanors are treated as principals and you are one. You tell the police officers you were only a passenger. Yes, you helped drink the beer. All right, you rode in a truck with gas you knew was stolen, and you sat in the car when Paul left it running to go get the beer—which Paul apparently stole—but you did not do anything. After your conversation with the investigating officers, you are taken to the police station and booked for two counts of petty larceny, and released to your mother's custody. You are to appear in city court to answer to the charges a week from Monday at 9:00 AM.

You finally talk to Paul, who apologizes for implicating you but says, "I had no choice." Paul suggests that you and he leave the state since the police will not come after you in another state just for a misdemeanor. You think about it, but you are in enough trouble as it is, and running away would not help anything. You were into some vandalism once before and a couple of incidents of shoplifting and nothing happened other than you had to make restitution, so you decide to go to court and take your chances.

Judge Ward, the city judge, has recently been elected to his post. He is a retired FBI agent who ran on a platform of "getting tough on crime." In fact, rumor has it that the judge has not uttered *not guilty* since he was elected. Sure enough, you appear in court, the judge listens to your case, and then thunders "I find you guilty"—believing himself hard, fair, incorruptible, and knowledgeable.

It was the worst day of your life. The judge deferred sentencing until the case worker submits a report. The case worker will interview you, your family, and some friends before making recommendations to the judge. You could be looking at 6 months in jail, a $500 fine, restitution, community service, and maybe more. You cannot believe all this happened to you because you hooked up with Paul on the 4th of July.

You decide to visit the public defender's office for help. Although public defenders in your state are required only to deal with felony cases, maybe you can get some advice. A legal intern in the public defender's office tells you honesty is the best policy and to cooperate with the case worker. You find out that the case worker is also a probation officer. You do not trust the intern's advice. "Say nothing; it is your constitutional right," says Paul. After an uncooperative interview, you receive a summons to appear in Judge Ward's chambers; the case worker will also be there.

The case worker's report is thorough. It touches on your past arrests, your uncooperativeness, and your denial of guilt. Judge Ward has a number of options: the fine, jail time, restitution probation, public service, or a new military-style training program designed to motivate and teach young offenders respect for authority. This is a federally sponsored program located on a nearby national guard base. What would you do if you were Judge Ward?

Questions for Discussion

A "short, sharp shock" may sometimes be an effective deterrent, but is incarceration for minor offenses a cost-effective method of punishment from either an economic or a social point of view? What corrective measures are most likely to instill a sense of responsibility in this youthful offender? You have read the options. What do you think is the most effective way to adjudicate this case and why? What would you hope for if you were the 18-year-old? If you were the 18-year-old's parents?

Case 3

Sexual Harassment

What a mess! You let out a deep sigh as you hang up the telephone. Sitting at your desk, staring out the window, you listen to the rain and slowly try to collect your thoughts.

Margot Williamson has just called you in tears. Three years ago she was part of your caseload. This time around she is assigned to Vic, your office supervisor. When Margot was originally assigned to you for case supervision, she had been convicted of drug possession and prostitution. You remember her well: an attractive 16-year-old black girl with a toddler daughter, a drug addition, a police record, and very little education. You worked with her for 2 years and watched her gradually dig her way out of the hole she had dug into a life with some hope. She earned a GED degree. With the help and support of a caring grandmother, she learned how to become a mother herself. When she finished her term of probation, she found a job in an upscale department store selling cosmetics and women's fashions. You felt her chances to make it were excellent. She seemed to have improved her sense of self-esteem and had dreams of one day owning and operating her own fashion boutique. Apparently something happened in the year following her release from probation. Who knows? Relapses happen. You have been in the business for 15 years and it still disappoints you when someone doesn't make it. What makes Margot's current situation even more frustrating is that it involves Vic, your supervisor.

Vic is white, 46 years old, and divorced. Margot has just tearfully informed you that Vic has grown increasingly aggressive over the last 3 months in trying to force her into a sexual relationship with him. Apparently it began with flattering comments about Margot's appearance and telling her that she was too pretty to be a prostitute. The harassment has now progressed to Vic offering to recommend unsupervised probation in exchange for sexual favors—and threatening her with revocation if she refuses his advances. You recall Margot's words,

"He told me that since I was a prostitute, it shouldn't be a big deal. He even offered me money if I was good enough."

You get a sick feeling in your stomach when you recall what she said. You have heard rumors about Vic. This probably isn't the first time he has done something like this. You have never seen any proof of the rumors, so you never accepted them as being true. Besides, Vic has always been good to you. Now you find yourself feeling angry and foolish. This time you are going to have to act. You gave Margot all the reassurance you could and promised to get back to her. You have to respond to this problem, but how? You consider calling Carl Baxter, the regional supervisor, but are uncertain since he and Vic are good friends. In fact, they play golf together every week. You also realize that getting caught in the middle of this problem can harm your own career. After all, you have a wife and children. Besides, Margot hasn't exactly been a model of virtue. She has brought a lot of this trouble on herself. Still, it isn't right for Vic to abuse his power over a client the way he has.

Questions for Discussion

How could sexism and racism be a part of Vic's harassment of Margot? Can you think of other potential problems in such settings involving racism and sexism? What about your responsibility as the probation officer caught in the middle? What could be the consequences of your taking action against Vic? Would it be better if you checked out the previous allegations against him? What are some safeguards that could be implemented to deter this type of harassment?

The Public Has a Right to Know

Overcrowding in correctional institutions has become a fact of life in many states. It is a consequence of tougher sentencing and parole laws, reduction in the age of criminal culpability for juveniles, and lagging community programs. Your state is no exception. As director of classification, you have tried every device you can think of to subclassify your inmates into groups according to their needs and the institution's requirement to provide a safe and healthy environment in which rehabilitation can be practiced while maintaining security. Your facility is a medium-security institution. With the population now at almost 40% over the original design capacity—and with the central office daily dumping more and more inmates into your office—the process of providing basic housing outweighs the need for selective assignment and treatment.

You have kept the warden fully aware of the classification problem. Space considerations are dictating the rules of classification; the hospital unit, in particular, is in crisis. Geriatric inmates are now more prevalent in the population, and they require more medical care with problems like renal failure, liver disease, cancer, and heart disease. In addition, there has been a huge influx of HIV-positive inmates, products of dirty needles and unprotected sex, that means you have no choice but to put chronically ill inmates into the general population, unless their symptoms are so severe that they cannot work and require ongoing care by medical personnel. Some new drugs seem to be helping with the pain and suffering of inmates with some diseases, but that does not solve the problem of dealing with the growing number of prisoners who require special medical attention.

You would prefer not to meet with Dan Short of the *Times Herald*. He has been assigned to write a series of articles on prison costs in response to some letters to the editor on the skyrocketing costs of medical services as reflected in the department of corrections budget just submitted to the legislature. The corrections budget now exceeds the budget for the community colleges. People do not seem to realize that persons incarcerated by the state have a right to safety and basic medical care just as much as people in the free world. It is two o'clock and time for Mr. Short's arrival. You wish you had all the answers—and most of all you wish the warden had handled this instead of you!

Bob Short's questions are what you would expect from a seasoned investigative journalist—well thought out, concise, and aimed directly at the heart of the problem. "How many persons are incarcerated here?" Short asks.

"Twenty-nine hundred and fifty-six," you respond, "depending on how many we gained or lost since 6:00 AM this morning." You want Short to know you are right on top of the problem.

"How many persons was this prison built to house?" Short continued.

"The original plans called for 2,000 beds, additional building has upped capacity to 2,300." You continue, "That may not seem like much, only 600 over, about 28%, and they all have bunks, but the programs are all messed up. We cannot do much 'correcting'; I'd like to know who coined that word, and certainly our rehabilitative and social programs are overwhelmed to the point of being ineffective. Overcrowding adversely affects everything—the staff, the inmates, all of their families—everything. But cope we must, and cope we will."

Short takes notes and remarks, "I think most people understand that prison overcrowding is a problem, but they do not understand the associated costs that come with it, like the program breakdowns and something you did not mention, medical costs." Short looked directly in your eyes—this is what he is after. "Let me ask you this," Short continues, "How many persons do you have here who are HIV positive, or do you test them?"

You respond, "About 10%; this morning there were six new cases diagnosed and reported. From diagnosis to release or death, as the case may be, our inmates are here for an average of 8 years. We figure we spend $18,000 per year on drugs and treatment for those with HIV. This is above the normal cost of incarceration."

"What is the normal cost?" Short probes.

You reply, "Hard to figure exactly because there are capital, brick and mortar costs, socioeconomic costs such as loss of income and income turnaround, family depending on public support, etc. But for an idea of the costs, you can take the population incarcerated and divide that into the annual appropriation, less capital improvements. That would be about $41,000 per inmate. That includes food, guard salaries, and so on, but it does not tell the whole story. It is just a number."

Short looks at you questioningly and comments, "Social costs are always hard to figure. They are full of counterbalancing variables—for example, if you did not have any prisoners, all the guards would be out of work. But let me get to the meat of this subject," Short continues.

"Your sick people, persons dying with cancer, the HIV group, your geriatric inmates, what do you do with them?"

"I wish you had not asked," you say. "Basically, they are in with the general population if they can manage. We do not have the room to set up special care programs for them. They will stay in the population until they cannot take care of their own needs, then they will go to the hospital and die. A few will be released before they die due to expiration of sentence. I wish we could do better, but with current inmate population trends, it looks like there is no end to the problem."

Short folds his notebook and says, "How about the governor—could he not release some of your sickest prisoners?"

"He could," you reply, "under his executive clemency powers he can commute, pardon, and reprieve, but he will not. He wants the scales of justice to apply equally to all regardless of age, health, or wealth."

Short prepares to leave the room, "I will not quote you because I know you cannot criticize the governor, but what would you do?"

You ponder Short's questions for the rest of your shift. What *would* you do, if you had the power?

Questions for Discussion

Conditions caused by prison overcrowding account for many of the lawsuits and other problems confronting prison administrators. The irony is that the cost to repair the deficit conditions may be less than the cost of defense of the lawsuits and the human costs arising from the years of neglect suffered by the corrections systems. How would you approach the problem of the sick, the elderly, and the HIV infected inmates? Consider integration, isolation, and early release as long-term measures. What would you do short term for expediency?

Case 5

Watch What You Say

As commissioner of corrections you are frequently invited to address various civic groups and other organizations. You enjoy these occasions for the most part. They are good public forums in which to discuss the goals of the department and brag about its successes. Recently, you addressed a noontime civic club meeting. Although you had not been aware that any members of the press were in attendance, it would not have mattered if you had known. You did not say anything that, in your opinion, was especially controversial. During a brief question-and-answer session at the end of your speech, you were asked to talk for a moment about a local news story that reported finding an inmate's social media page that apparently was being updated using a cell phone inside the prison. Your response included an admission that contraband does, in fact, sometimes make its way inside the prison, a description of the security protocols in place to uncover contraband, and your view that the media was over sensationalizing the frequency of cell phones in prisons based on this one incident. Finally, you mention that prison crowding makes it difficult to control contraband, especially with current staffing levels.

The next day, the local newspaper ran a somewhat dramatic editorial stating that you had denied responsibility for the cell phones and that you instead blamed the media for running the story. That afternoon you received a phone call from an extremely irate Lester Knowles, chairman of the Senate Committee on Penitentiaries. He reminded you in no uncertain terms that your job was to enforce policies, not make them. Later that day, another senator, Sue Atkins, who is head of a task force on correctional reform, also contacted you to request that you advise her and her blue-ribbon panel on the topic of correctional alternatives. Since you were a former probation officer at the start of your career, you have been on both sides of the fence. While you are confident that you could offer substantial insight to Senator

Atkins' task force, you know you would be doing so at your own peril: you also realize that Senator Knowles would definitely not approve.

Questions for Discussion

Prison overcrowding may or may not be a problem for Senator Knowles or the governor, but it is a real and pressing problem in your world. How do you respond to two senators who have conflicting interests and priorities? What is the right course of action for you to take?

Case 6

Outsourcing for Profit

The Department of Corrections decided several years ago to contract out to a private vendor for inmate medical services. As superintendent of a large institution, you have had more than a few occasions to cast a critical eye toward the medical care being provided by the contractor. You receive a phone call early Saturday morning from the distressed wife of an inmate. Another inmate had called to tell her that at 6:00 AM her husband had been taken to the prison hospital suffering from what appeared to be a stroke. You calmed the inmate's wife down and assured her you would check on her husband.

Arriving at the hospital at 8:15, you found the inmate in an examination room, unattended. He was unable to converse very well as his speech was slurred. The left side of his face was drooping, and he indicated he could not move his left arm. You found a nurse and inquired about the inmate's condition. She said he had "probably suffered a stroke but they wouldn't know for sure until the doctor examined him." You looked at your watch and asked if, in fact, the inmate had been waiting two hours and still had not seen a doctor. The nurse replied that on Saturdays the doctor usually came in late unless there was an emergency!

Angrily, you called the company's regional director at home and explained the situation. You argue that the prison is required to provide adequate medical care to inmates. The regional director responded that the courts have been very reluctant to intervene in these situations over the past decade, and he believes that any lawsuit regarding the quality of medical care would be dismissed. He indicated that if you wanted a physician on duty on weekends, it would cost the department additional money.

Questions for Discussion

Who has the authority to address deficiencies when medical care is privatized? How can increasing efficiency regarding financial savings for the corrections department result in increased human costs? What is a proper balance between maintaining fiscal responsibility and inmate health care?

Case 7

The Last Meal

You have been a warden for more than a decade, serving at several different institutions. Most recently, you were transferred to the state's highest-security prison that houses Death Row. Although you have not carried out any executions since becoming a warden, you did serve on an execution team while a deputy warden. While serving on that team, you once had to carry out an execution of an inmate in which there were real questions about the man's innocence. Needless to say, carrying out executions is something that you have been dreading since being promoted to warden.

Just a week ago you were served with a death warrant for prisoner Clyde Prescott, who has been on death row for nearly 15 years. The attorney general advises you that barring any unforeseen last minute legal problems, the execution will be "a go." You immediately begin addressing the many aspects of the protocol to be followed in preparation for the execution. One of these details involves the inmate's last meal; the inmate can choose the menu, and the meal will be served during an extended visitation from family. Your previous experience on the execution team showed you that this gesture of compassion goes a long way in helping the offender cope with their impending execution.

The governor just called your office and stated emphatically that she does not want inmates to have the privilege of special last meals while awaiting execution. She sees this as an extra expense and a sign of disrespect toward the victim's family. After you express your disagreement, the governor tells you that she will move to cut next year's budget if you do not comply with her demands.

Questions for Discussion

How do you balance the governor's demand with the compassion of offering the inmate the choice of a last meal? Are there any compromises available that would allow extended visitation while following the governor's request? If so, what should the protocol be for that compromise?

186

References

Ahlin, E. M., Hagen, C. A., Harmon, M. A., & Crosse, S. (2016). Kiosk reporting among probationers in the United States. *The Prison Journal, 96*(5), 688–708.

Amnesty International. (2017). The global view. Retrieved from https://www.Amnesty.org/en/what-we-do/death-penalty/

Andersen, L., & Andersen, S. (2014). Effect of electronic monitoring on social welfare dependence. *Criminology & Public Policy, 13*(3), 349–379.

Armstrong, G. S., Atkin-Plunk, C. A., & Wells, J. (2015). The relationship between work-family conflict, correctional officer job stress, and job satisfaction. *Criminal Justice and Behavior, 42*(10), 1066–1082.

Atkin, C. A., & Armstrong, G. S. (2013). Does the concentration of parolees in a community impact employer attitudes toward the hiring of ex-offenders? *Criminal Justice Policy Review, 24*, 71–93.

Austin, J., Cadora, E., Clear, T. R., Dansky, K., Greene, J., Gupta, V., Mauer, M., Porter, N., Tucker, S., Young, M.C. (2013). *Ending mass incarceration: Charting a new justice reinvestment.* Washington, DC: The Sentencing Project.

Aviram, H., & Newby, R. (2013). Death row economics: The rise of fiscally prudent anti-death penalty activism. *Criminal Justice, 28*, 33–40.

Barrett, D. E., Ju, S., Katsiyannis, A., & Zhang, D. (2015). Females in the juvenile justice system: Influences on delinquency and recidivism. *Journal of Child and Family Studies, 24*, 427–433.

Baxter v. Palmigiano, 425 US 308 (1976).

Baze v. Rees, 533 US 35 (2008).

Beard v. Banks, 548 US 521 (2006).

Bechard, S., Ireland, C., Berg, B., & Vogel, B. (2011). Arbitrary arbitration: Diverting juveniles into the justice system: A reexamination after 22 years. *International Journal of Offender Therapy and Comparative Criminology, 55*(4), 605–625.

Beck, A. J., Berzofsky, M., Caspar, R., & Krebs, C. (2013). *Sexual victimization in prisons and jails reported by inmates, 2011–12.* Bureau of Justice Statistics. Washington, DC: U.S. Department of Justice.

Bell v. Wolfish, 441 US 520 (1979).

Berger, E. (2014). Lethal injection secrecy and Eighth Amendment due process. *Boston College Law Review, 55*(5), 367–1441.

Block v. Rutherford, 468 US 576 (1984).

Bodenhorn, H. (2016). Prison crowding, recidivism, and early release in early Rhode Island. *Explorations in Economic History, 59*, 55–74.

Bohm, R. M. (2017). *Deathquest: An introduction to the theory and practice of capital punishment in the United States*. New York, NY: Routledge.

Bounds v. Smith, 430 US 817 (1976).

Brazzell, D., Crayton, A., Mukamal, D. A., Solomon, A. L., & Lindahl, N. (2009). *From the classroom to the community: Exploring the role of education during incarceration and reentry*. Washington, DC: The Urban Institute.

Bright, S. (2015). The role of race, poverty, intellectual disability, and mental illness in the decline of the death penalty. *University of Richmond Law Review, 49*, 671–692.

Bronson, J., & Berzofsky, M. (2017). *Indicators of mental health problems reported by prisoners and jail inmates, 2011–12*. Bureau of Justice Statistics. Washington, DC: U.S. Department of Justice.

Bronson, J., Stroop, J., Zimmer, S., & Berzofsky, M. (2017). *Drug use, dependence, and abuse among state prisoners and jail inmates, 2007–2009*. Bureau of Justice Statistics. Washington, DC: U.S. Department of Justice.

Brown v. Plata, 563 US 493 (2011).

Bureau of Justice Statistics. (2005). *Census of state and federal adult correctional facilities, 2005*. Washington, DC: U.S. Department of justice.

Bureau of Labor Statistics. (2018, March). Occupational employment statistics: Correctional officers and jailers. Washington, DC: Department of Labor. Retrieved from https://www.bls.gov/oes/current/oes333012.htm

Bureau of Labor Statistics. (2018, March). Occupational employment statistics: Probation officers and correctional treatment specialists. Washington, DC: Department of Labor. Retrieved from https://www.bls.gov/oes/current/oes211092.htm#st

Burke, P., Herman, P., Stroker, R., & Giguere, R. (2010). *TPC case management handbook: An integrated case management approach*. Washington, DC: National Institute of Corrections.

Burkhardt, B. C., & Jones, A. (2016). Judicial intervention into prisons: Comparing private and public prisons from 1990 to 2005. *Justice System Journal, 37*, 39–52.

Butler, H. D., Griffin, O. H., III., & Johnson, W. W. (2012). What makes you the worst of the worst? An examination of state policies defining supermaximum confinement. *Criminal Justice Policy Review, 24*(6), 676–694.

Camilletti, C. (2010). *Pretrial diversion program: Research summary*. Washington, DC: Bureau of Justice Assistance.

Cantora, A. (2015). Navigating the job search after incarceration: The experiences of work-release participants. *Criminal Justice Studies, 28*(2), 141–160.

CAPI [Center for the Advancement of Public Integrity]. (2016, September). *Prison corruption: The problem and some potential solutions*. New York, NY: Columbia Law School.

Carson, E. A. (2018). *Prisoners in 2016*. Washington, DC: Bureau of Justice Statistics.

Carson, E. A., & Sabol, W. J. (2016). *Aging of the state prison population, 1993–2013*. Bureau of Justice Statistics Special Report. Washington, DC: U.S. Department of Justice.

Center for Health & Justice at TASC. (2013). *No entry: A national survey of criminal justice diversion programs and initiatives.* Chicago, IL: Author.

Cheeseman, K. A., & Downey, R. A. (2012). Talking 'bout my generation: The effect of "generation" on correctional employee perceptions of work stress and job satisfaction. *The Prison Journal, 92*, 24–44.

Cihan, A., Davidson, M., & Sorensen, J. (2017). Analyzing the heterogeneous nature of inmate behavior: Trajectories of prison misconduct. *The Prison Journal, 97*(4), 431–450.

Cobbina, J. E., Huebner, B. M., & Berg, M. T. (2012). Men, women, and postrelease offending: An examination of the nature of the link between relational ties and recidivism. *Crime & Delinquency, 58*(3), 331–361.

Cochran, J. C., Mears, D. P., & Bales, W. D. (2017). Who gets visited in prison? Individual-and community-level disparities in inmate visitation experiences. *Crime & Delinquency, 63*(5), 545–568.

Coker v. Georgia, 97 S.Ct. 2861, 433 US 584 (1977).

Cooper v. Pate, 378 US 546 (1964).

Courtney, L., Eppler-Epstein, S., Pelletier, E., King, R., & Lei, S. (2017, July). *A matter of time: The causes and consequences of rising time served in America's prisons.* The Urban Institute. Retrieved from http://apps.urban.org/features/long-prison-terms/intro.html

Crank, B. R., & Brezina, T. (2013). Prison will either make ya or break ya: Punishment, deterrence, and the criminal lifestyle. *Deviant Behavior, 34*, 782–802.

Cruz v. Beto, 405 US 319 (1971).

Cui, G. (2016). Evidence-based sentencing and the taint of dangerousness. *Yale Law Journal, 125.*

Cutter v. Wilkinson, 544 US 709 (2005).

Davis, L. M., Steele, J. L., Bozick, R., Williams, M. V., Turner, S., Miles, J. N. V., Saunders, J., & Steinberg, P. S. (2014). *How effective is correctional education, and where do we go from here? The results of a comprehensive evaluation.* Washington, DC: Rand Corporation.

Death Penalty Information Center. (2018, April 30). Facts about the death penalty. Washington, DC: Author.

Delaney, T. (2016). Sports, leisure, and recreation in prison. In Delaney, T. (Ed.), *Sportsmanship: Multidisciplinary perspectives* (pp. 53–65). Jefferson, NC: McFarland & Company.

DeMichele, M. (2014). Electronic monitoring: It is a tool, not a silver bullet. *Criminology & Public Policy, 13*(3), 393–400.

Denney, A. S., & Tewksbury, R. (2013). Motivations and the need for fulfillment of faith-based halfway house volunteers. *Justice Policy Journal, 10*, 1–24.

Dial, K. C. (2010). *Stress and the correctional officer.* El Paso, TX: LFB Scholarly Publishing.

Dial, K. C., Downey, R. A., & Goodlin, W. E. (2010). The job in the joint: The impact of generation and gender on work stress in prison. *Journal of Criminal Justice, 38*(4), 609–615.

Duwe, G. (2017, June). The use and impact of correctional programming for inmates on pre- and post-release outcomes. Washington, DC: National Institute of Justice.

Duwe, G., & Clark, V. (2011). Blessed be the social tie that binds: The effects of prison visitation on offender recidivism. *Criminal Justice Policy Review, 24*(3), 271–296.

Duwe, G., & Clark, V. (2013). The effects of private prison confinement on offender recidivism: Evidence from Minnesota. *Criminal Justice Review, 38*(3), 375–394.

Duwe, G., & Johnson, B. R. (2016). The effects of prison visits from community volunteers on offender recidivism. *The Prison Journal, 96*(2), 279–303.

Duwe, G., & King, M. (2012). Can faith-based correctional programs work? An outcome evaluation of the innerchange freedom initiative in Minnesota. *International Journal of Offender Therapy and Comparative Criminology, 57*(7), 813–841.

Edwards, B. D., & Pealer, J. (2018). *Policing special needs offenders: Implementing training to improve police-citizen encounters.* New York, NY: Routledge.

Ellis, H., & Alexander, V. (2017). The mentally ill in jail: Contemporary clinical and practice perspectives for psychiatric-mental health nursing. *Archives of Psychiatric Nursing, 31*, 217–222.

Epperson, M. W., Thompson, J. G., Lurigio, A. J., & Kim, S. (2017). Unpacking the relationship between probationers with serious mental illnesses and probation officers: A mixed-methods examination. *Journal of Offender Rehabilitation, 56*(3), 188–216.

Estelle v. Gamble, 429 US 97 (1976).

Ewert, S., & Wildhagen, T. (2011). *Educational characteristics of prisoners: Data from the ACS.* Washington, DC: U.S. Census Bureau, Housing and Household Economic Statistics Division.

Farmer v. Brennan, 511 US 825 (1994).

Fins, D. (2017). *Death row USA: Summer 2017.* NAACP Criminal Justice Project. Retrieved from: http://www.naacpldf.org/files/case_issue/DRUSASummer2017.pdf

Fleury-Steiner, B., & Longazel, J. (2014). *The pains of mass imprisonment.* New York, NY: Routledge.

Freiburger, T. L., & Hilinski, C. M. (2011). Probation officers' recommendations and final sentencing outcomes. *Journal of Crime and Justice, 34*, 45–61.

Furman v. Georgia, 408 US 238 (1972).

Gagnon v. Scarpelli, 411 US 778 (1973).

Garland, B., & Wilson, G. (2012). Prison inmates' views of whether reporting rape is the same as snitching: An exploratory study and research agenda. *Journal of Interpersonal Violence, 28*(6), 1201–1222.

Garland, B., & Hass, A. Y. (2015). An outcome evaluation of a Midwestern prisoner reentry initiative. *Criminal Justice Policy Review, 26*(3), 293–314.

Garland, B., Wodahl, E., & Schuhmann, R. (2013). Value conflict and public opinion toward prisoner reentry initiatives. *Criminal Justice Policy Review, 2*, 27–48.

Gehrke, J. (2017, Oct. 3). State department defends US vote against death penalty ban at the UN. *Washington Examiner.* Retrieved from http://www.washingtonexaminer.com/state-department-defends-us-vote-against-death-penalty-ban-at-the-un/article/2636429

Glossip v. Gross, 576 US ___ (2015).

Goffman, E. (1961). *Asylums: Essays on the social situation of mental patients and other inmates.* Garden City, CA: Anchor Books.

Gordon, J., & Baker, T. (2017). Examining correctional officers' fear of victimization by inmates: The influence of fear facilitators and fear inhibitors. *Criminal Justice Policy Review, 28*(5), 462–487.

Gould, D. D., Watson, S. L., Price, S. R., & Valliant, P. M. (2012). The relationship between burnout and coping in adult and young offender center correctional officers: An exploratory investigation. *Psychological Services, 10*, 37–47.

Gregg v. Georgia, 428 US 158 (1976).

Griffin, M. L., & Hepburn, J. R. (2013). Inmate misconduct and the institutional capacity for control. *Criminal Justice and Behavior, 40*(3), 270–288.

Griffin, M. L., Hogan, N. L., Lambert, E. G., Tucker-Gail, K. A., & Baker, D. N. (2010). Job involvement, job stress, job satisfaction, and organizational commitment and the burnout of correctional staff. *Criminal Justice and Behavior, 37*(2), 239–255.

Grim, R. (2016, April 14). Mississippi jails are losing inmates, and local officials are devastated by the loss of revenue. *Huffington Post*. Retrieved from https://www.huffingtonpost.com/entry/mississippi-jails-revenue_us_57100da1e4b06f35cb6f14e8

Gross, S. (2012). Baldus and the legacy of *McCleskey v. Kemp. Iowa Law Review, 97*, 1905–1924.

Harcourt, B. (2015). Risk as a proxy for race: The dangers of risk assessment. *Federal Sentencing Reporter, 27*, 237–243

Hartley, D. J., Davila, M. A., Marquart, J. W., & Mullings, J. L. (2013). Fear is a disease: The impact of fear and exposure to infectious disease on correctional officer job stress and satisfaction. *American Journal of Criminal Justice, 38*, 323–340.

Hawkins, I., & Scherr, K. (2017). Engaging the CSI effect: The influences of experience-taking, type of evidence, and viewing frequency on juror decision-making. *Journal of Criminal Justice, 49*, 45–52.

Haynes, S. H., Cares, A. C., & Ruback, R. B. (2015). Reducing the harm of criminal victimization: The role of restitution. *Violence and Victims, 30*(3), 450–469.

Haywood v. Drown et al., 556 US__ (2009).

Helling v. McKinney, 509 US 25 (1993).

Hewitt v. Helms, 459 US 460 (1983)

Hockenberry, S., & Puzzanchera, C. (2017). *Juvenile court statistics, 2014.* Pittsburg, PA: National Center for Juvenile Justice.

Hoffman, H. C., & Dickinson, G. E. (2011). Characteristics of prison hospice programs in the United States. *American Journal of Hospice & Palliative Medicine, 28*(4), 245–252.

Holt v. Hobbs, 574 US__ (2015).

Hudson v. McMillian, 503 US 1 (1992).

Hudson v. Palmer, 468 US 517 (1984).

Hutto v. Finney, 437 US 678 (1978).

In re Gault. (1967). 387 U.S. 1.

Irwin, J., & Cressey, D. R. (1962). Thieves, convicts and the inmate culture. *Social Problems, 10*(2), 142–155.

Jacobs, J. B., & Olitsky, E. (2012, May 16). The importance of correctional leadership. *CorrectionsOne*. Retrieved from https://www.correctionsone.com/jail-management/articles/5582170-The-importance-of-correctional-leadership/

Johnson v. Avery, 393 US 483 (1969).

Johnson v. California, 543 US 499 (2005).

Johnson, R., & Dobrzanska, A. (2005). Mature coping among life-sentenced inmates: An exploratory study of adjustment dynamics. *Corrections Compendium, 30*(6), 8–9, 36–38.

Johnson, R., Rocheleau, A. M., & Martin, A. B. (2017). *Hard time: A fresh look at understanding and reforming the prison* (4th ed.). Madden, MA: John Wiley & Sons.

Jones v. Bock, 549 US 199 (2007).

Kaeble, D. & Cowhig, M. (2018). *Correctional populations in the United States, 2016*. Washington, DC: Bureau of Justice Statistics.

Kang-Brown, J., & Subramanian, R. (2017). *Out of sight: The growth of jails in rural America*. New York, NY: Vera Institute of Justice.

Kappeler, V., & Potter, G. (2018). *The mythology of crime and criminal justice* (5th ed.). Long Grove, IL: Waveland Press.

Karsten, J., & West, D. (2017, September 21). Decades later, electronic monitoring of offenders is still prone to failure. Washington, DC: The Brookings Institution.

Kentucky Department of Corrections v. Thompson, 490 US 454 (1989).

Kerle, K. (2016). The mentally ill and crisis intervention teams: Reflections on jails and the U.S. mental health challenge. *The Prison Journal, 96*, 153–161.

Kerley, K. R., & Copes, H. (2008). "Keepin' my mind right": Identity maintenance and religious social support in the prison context. *International Journal of Offender Therapy and Comparative Criminology, 53*, 228–244.

Kort-Butler, L., & Malone, S. E. (2015). Citizen volunteers in prison: Bringing the outside in, taking the inside out. *Journal of Crime and Justice, 38*(4), 508–521.

Lambert, E. G., Barton-Bellessa, S. M., & Hogan, N. L. (2015). The consequences of emotional burnout among correctional staff. *SAGE Open, 5*(2), 1–15.

Lambert, E. G., Worley, R., & Worley, V. B. (2018, April). The effects of perceptions of staff-inmate boundary violations and willingness to follow rules upon work stress. *Security Journal, 31*, 618–644.

Landess, J. (2016). Civil and constitutional rights of adjudicated youth. *Child and Adolescent Psychiatric Clinics, 25*, 19–26.

Latessa, E. J., & Smith, P. (2015). *Corrections in the community* (6th ed.). New York, NY: Routledge.

LaVigne, N., Bieler, S., Cramer, L., Ho, H., Kotonias, C., Mayer, D., McClure, D., Pacifici, L., Parks, E., Peterson, B., & Samuels, J. (2014). *Justice reinvestment initiative state assessment report*. Washington, DC: Urban Institute.

Lee v. Washington, 390 US 333 (1968).

Leigey, M. E., & Ryder, M. A. (2015). The pains of permanent imprisonment: Examining perceptions of confinement among older life without parole inmates. *International Journal of Comparative Criminology, 59*(7), 726–742.

Leigey, M. E. (2015). *The forgotten men: Serving a life without parole sentence*. New Brunswick, NJ: Rutgers University Press.

Leone, P., & Weinberg, L. (2012). *Addressing the unmet educational needs of children and youth in the juvenile justice and child welfare systems*. Washington, DC: Center for Juvenile Justice Reform.

Lerman, A. E., & Page, J. (2012). The state of the job: An embedded work role perspective on prison officer attitudes. *Punishment & Society, 14*(5), 503–529.

Lewis v. Smith, 518 US 343 (1996).

Lieberman, J. D. (2011). The utility of scientific jury selection: Still murky after 30 years. *Current Directions in Psychological Science, 20*, 48–52.

Lindsey, A. M., Mears, D. P., & Cochran, J. C. (2016). The privatization debate: A conceptual framework for improving (public and private) corrections. *Journal of Contemporary Criminal Justice, 32*(4), 308–327.

Listwan, S. J., Sullivan, C. J., Agnew, R., Cullen, F. T., & Colvin, M. (2013). The pains of imprisonment revisited: The impact of strain on inmate recidivism. *Justice Quarterly, 30*, 144–168.

Louden, J. E., Skeem, J. L., Camp, J., Vidal, S., & Peterson, J. (2012). Supervision practices in specialty mental health probation: What happens in officer-probationer meetings? *Law and Human Behavior, 36*(2), 109–119.

Lundahl, B. W., Kunz, C., Brownell, C., Harris, N., & Vleet, R. V. (2009). Prison privatization: A meta-analysis of cost and quality of confinement indicators. *Research on Social Work Practice, 19*(4), 383–394.

MacKenzie, D. L. (2012). The effectiveness of corrections-based work and academic and vocational education programs (pp. 492–520). In J. Petersilia & K. Reitz (Eds.), *The Oxford handbook of sentencing and corrections*. New York, NY: Oxford University Press.

Makarios, M. D., & Maahs, J. (2012). Is private time quality time? A national private-public comparison of prison quality. *The Prison Journal, 92*(3), 336–357.

Manchak, S. M., Skeem, J. L., Kennealy, P. J., & Louden, J. E. (2014). High-fidelity specialty mental health probation improves officer practices, treatment access, and rule compliance. *Law and Human Behavior, 38*, 450–461.

Marceau, J., & Chen, A. (2014, September 27). The continuing problems with lethal injection. *Huffington Post*.

Marcum, C. D., Hilinski-Rosick, C. M., & Freiburger, T. L. (2014). Examining the correlates of male and female inmate misconduct. *Security Journal, 27*(3), 284–303.

Martin, G. (2012). Marching upstream. In M. Mauer & K. Epstein (Eds.), *To build a better criminal justice system: 25 experts envision the next 25 years of reform* (pp. 48–49). Washington, DC: The Sentencing Project.

Martin, J. L., Lichtenstein, B., Jenkot, R. B., & Forde, D. R. (2012). "They can take us over any time they want": Correctional officers' responses to prison crowding. *The Prison Journal, 92*, 88–105.

McCarthy v. Madigan, 503 US 140 (1992).

McCarthy, B. J., & Perry-Bellmer, C. J. (2017). Keeping an eye on the keeper: The impact of corrupt practices on the prison. In M. Braswell, B. McCarthy, & B. McCarthy (Eds.), *Justice, crime and ethics* (pp. 292–314). New York, NY: Routledge.

McCleskey v. Kemp, 481 US 279 (1987).

McMurran, M. (2009). Motivational interviewing with offenders: A systematic review. *Legal and Criminological Psychology, 14*, 83–100.

Meachum v. Fano, 427 US 216 (1976) (1976).

Mears, D. P. (2013). Supermax prisons: The policy and the evidence. *Criminology & Public Policy, 12*(4), 681–712.

Mears, D. P. (2017). *Out-of-control criminal justice*. New York, NY: Cambridge University Press.

Mears, D., Cochran, J. C., & Bales, W. (2012). Gender differences in the effects of prison on recidivism. *Journal of Criminal Justice, 40*, 370–378.

Merlo, A. V., & Benekos, P. J. (2017). *Reaffirming juvenile justice: From Gault to Montgomery*. New York, NY: Routledge.

Millbrook v. United States, 569 US__ (2013).

Miller, J. A. (2010). Sex offender civil commitment: The treatment paradox. *California Law Review, 98*(6), 2093–2128.

Miller, K. L. (2010). The darkest figure of crime: Perceptions of reasons for male inmates to not report sexual assault. *Justice Quarterly, 27*(5), 692–712.

Miller, W. R. (1983). Motivational interviewing with problem drinkers. *Behavioural Psychotherapy*, 11, 147–172.

Miller, W. R., & Rollnick, S. (2013). *Motivational interviewing: Helping people change* (3rd ed.). New York, NY: The Guilford Pres.

Monroe v. Pape, 365 US 167 (1961).

Moore, K., Stuewig, J., & Tangney, J. (2013). Jail inmates' perceived and anticipated stigma: Implications for post-release functioning. *Self Identity, 15*(5), 527–547.

Morash, M., Jeong, S., Bohmert, M. N., & Bush, D. (2012). Men's vulnerability to prisoner-on-prisoner sexual violence: A state correctional system case study. *The Prison Journal, 92*(2), 290–311.

Morrisey v. Brewer, 408 US 471 (1972).

Murray v. Giarratano, 492 US 1 (1989).

Mushlin, M. B. & Galt, N. R. (2009). Getting real about race and prisoner rights. *Fordham Urban Law Journal, 36*, 27–52.

Nellis, A. (2017). *Still life: America's increasing use of life and long-term sentences*. Washington, DC: The Sentencing Project.

Newman v. Alabama, 438 US 781 (1977).

Noonan, M. E. (2016). *Mortality in state prisons, 2001–2014.* Bureau of Justice Statistics. Washington: DC: U.S. Department of Justice.

Nowotny, K. M., Cepeda, A., James-Hawkins, L., & Boardman, J. D. (2016). Growing old behind bars: Health profiles of the older male inmate population in the United States. *Journal of Aging and Health, 28*(6), 935–956.

O'lone v. Estate of Shabazz, 482 US 709 (1987).

Ono, N. (2016, October 27). Successful reentry: Partnerships on outside critical for ex-offenders making new start. Sacramento: California Forward. Retrieved from http://cafwd.org/reporting/entry-new/successful-reentry-partnerships-on-outside-critical-for-ex-offenders-making

Overton v. Bazzetta, 539 US 126 (2003).

Palmer, J. W. (2015). *Constitutional rights of prisoners* (9th ed.). New York, NY: Routledge.

Pennsylvania Department of Corrections v. Yeskey, 524 US 206 (1998).

Penrod, J., Loeb, S. J., & Smith, C. A. (2014). Administrators' perspectives on changing practice in end-of-life care in a state prison system. *Public Health Nursing, 31*(2), 99–108.

Pew Charitable Trusts. (2016). *Use of electronic offender-tracking devices expands sharply.* Retrieved from http://www.pewtrusts.org/en/research-and-analysis/issue-briefs/2016/09/use-of-electronic-offender-tracking-devices-expands-sharply

Phelps, M. S. (2012). The place of punishment: Variation in the provision of inmate services staff across the punitive turn. *Journal of Criminal Justice, 40*(5), 348–357.

Pogrebin, M., West-Smith, M., Walker, A., & Unnithan, N. P. (2014). Employment isn't enough: Financial obstacles experienced by ex-prisoners during the reentry process. *Criminal Justice Review, 39*(4), 394–410.

Porter v. Nussle, 534 US 516 (2002).

Powers, R. A., Kaukinen, C., & Jeanis, M. (2017). An examination of recidivism among inmates released from a private reentry center and public institutions in Colorado. *The Prison Journal, 97*(5), 609–627.

Procunier v. Martinez, 416 US 396 (1974).

Radelet, M. L., & Lacock, T. L. (2009). Do executions lower homicide rates? The views of leading criminologists. *Journal of Criminal Law & Criminology, 99*(2), 489–508.

Ramirez, M. D. (2013). Americans' changing views on crime and punishment. *Public Opinion Quarterly, 77*(4), 1006–1031.

Randol, B. M., & Campbell, C. M. (2017). Macro-correlates of inmate violence: The importance of programming in prison order. *The Prison Journal, 97*(4), 451–474.

Rembert, D. A., & Henderson, H. (2014). Correctional officer excessive use of force: Civil liability under section 1983. *The Prison Journal, 94*(2), 198–219.

Rhine, E., Petersilia, J., & Reitz, K. (2015). Improving parole release in America. *Federal Sentencing Reporter, 28*(2), 96–104.

Rhodes v. Chapman, 452 US 337 (1981).

Richmond, K. M. (2014). Why work while incarcerated? Inmate perceptions on prison industries employment. *Journal of Offender Rehabilitation, 53*, 231–252.

Rocheleau, A. M. (2013). An empirical exploration of the "pains of imprisonment" and the level of prison misconduct and violence. *Criminal Justice Review, 38*(3), 354–374.

Ross, J. I. (2013). Deconstructing correctional officer deviance: Toward typologies of actions and controls. *Criminal Justice Review, 38*, 110–126.

Ross, J. I., Tewksbury, R., & Rolfe, S. (2016). Inmate responses to correctional officer deviance: A model of its dynamic nature. *Corrections, 1*, 139–153.

Sandin v. Conner, 515 US 472 (1995).

Sarnoff, S. (2014). Restitution: Exploring disparities and potentials. *Criminology & Public Policy, 13*(3), 437–440.

Scaggs, S. A., & Bales, W. D. (2015). The growth in the elderly inmate prison population: The role of determinate punishment policies. *Justice Research and Policy, 16*, 99–118.

Schwalbe, C. S., Gearing, R. E., Mackenzie, M. J., Brewer, K. B., & Ibrahim, R. (2012). A meta-analysis of experimental studies of diversion programs for juvenile offenders. *Clinical Psychology Review, 32*, 26–33.

Seiter, R. P. (2017). *Correctional administration: Integrating theory and practice* (3rd ed.). Boston, MA: Pearson.

Sentencing Project. (2017). *Private prisons in the United States*. Washington, DC: Author.

Shah, R. S., Fine, L., & Gullen, J. (2014). *Juvenile records: A national review of state laws on confidentiality, sealing and expungement*. Philadelphia, PA: Juvenile Law Center.

Shannon, S., & Uggen, C. (2012). Incarceration as a political institution. In E. Amenta, K. Nash, & A. Scott (Eds.), *The Wiley-Blackwell companion to political sociology* (pp. 214–225). Malden, MA: John Wiley & Sons.

Shapiro, D. (2017, May 16). Sessions' moves revive allegations of past racism. *Chicago Tribune*, p. 15.

Shaw v. Murphy, 532 US 223 (2001).

Shelden, R., & Troshynski, E. (2019). *Delinquency and juvenile justice in American society* (3rd ed.). Long Grove, IL: Waveland Press.

Shelden, R., Brown, W., Miller, K., & Fritzler, R. (2016). *Crime and criminal justice in American society* (2nd ed.). Long Grove, IL: Waveland Press.

Shepard, S. P. (2011). Negligent hiring liability: A look at how it affects employers and the rehabilitation and reintegration of ex-offenders. *Appalachian Journal of Law, 10*, 145–182.

Simon, J. (2014). *Mass incarceration on trial: A remarkable court decision and the future of prisons in America*. New York, NY: The New Press.

Sireci v. Florida, 580 US ___ (2016).

Smokowski, P., Rose, R., Evans, C., Barbee, J., Cotter, K., & Bower, M. (2017). The impact of teen court on rural adolescents: Improved social relationships, psychological functioning, and school experiences. *Journal of Primary Prevention, 38*(4), 447–464.

Somin, I. (2014). Jury ignorance and political ignorance. *William & Mary Law Review, 55*, 1167–1193.

Spohr, S. A., Taxman, F. S., Rodriguez, M., & Walters, S. T. (2016). Motivational interviewing fidelity in a community corrections setting: Treatment initiation and subsequent drug use. *Journal of Substance Abuse Treatment, 65*, 20–25.

Starr, S. (2014a). Evidence-based sentencing and the scientific rationalization of discrimination. *Stanford Law Review, 66*, 803–872.

Starr, S. (2015). The new profiling: Why punishing based on poverty and identity is unconstitutional and wrong. *Federal Sentencing Reporter, 27*, 229–236.

Steiner, B., Ellison, J. M., Butler, H. D., & Cain, C. M. (2017). The impact of inmate and prison characteristics on prison victimization. *Trauma, Violence, & Abuse, 18*, 17–36.

Steiner, B., & Wooldredge, J. (2015). Individual and environmental sources of work stress among prison officers. *Criminal Justice and Behavior, 42*(8), 800–818.

Steiner, B., & Wooldredge, J. (2017). Individual and environmental influences on prison officer safety. *Justice Quarterly, 34*(2), 324–349.

Stephan, J. J. (2008). *Census of state and federal correctional facilities, 2005.* Bureau of Justice Statistics. Washington, DC: U.S. Department of Justice.

Stohr, M. K., & Walsh, A. (2018). *Corrections: From research, to policy, to practice*. Thousand Oaks, CA: Sage Publications.

Stohr, M. K., & Walsh, A. (2019). *Corrections: The essentials* (3rd ed.). Thousand Oaks, CA: Sage Publications.

Struckman-Johnson, C., & Struckman-Johnson, D. (2013). Stopping prison rape: The evolution of standards recommended by PREA's national prison rape elimination commission. *The Prison Journal, 93*(3), 335–354.

Sullivan, J. (2000, January 30). States and cities removing prisons from courts' grip. *The New York Times*.

Sun, K. (2013). *Correctional counseling: A cognitive growth perspective* (2nd ed.). Burlington, MA: Jones & Bartlett.

Superintendent v. Hill, 472 US 445 (1985).

Surette, R. (2015). *Media, crime, and criminal justice: Images, realities, and policies* (5th ed.). Stamford, CT: Cengage.

Swavola, E., Riley, K., & Subramanian, R. (2016). *Overlooked: Women and jails in an era of reform*. New York, NY: Vera Institute of Justice.

Sykes, G. M. (1958). *The society of captives*. Princeton, NJ: Princeton University Press.

Teigen, A. (2017). Juvenile age of jurisdiction and transfer to adult court laws. Denver, CO and Washington, DC: National Conference of State Legislatures.

Tepperman, A. (2014). Prison weights for no man: Interpreting a modern moral panic. *Critical Issues in Justice and Politics, 7*(1), 1–16.

The Council of State Governments Justice Center. (2015). *Locked out: Improving educational and vocational outcomes for incarcerated youth.* New York, NY: Author.

Thompson, D. (2015, Feb. 17). Sex offenders are being killed off in California prisons. *Business Insider.* Retrieved from http://www.businessinsider.com/sex-offenders-are-being-killed-off-in-california-prisons-2015-2

Thornburgh v. Abbott, 490 US 401 (1989).

Tonry, M. (2013). Sentencing in America, 1975–2025. *Crime and Justice, 42,* 141–198.

Topitzes, J., Mersky, J. P., & Reynolds, A. J. (2012). From child maltreatment to violent offending: An examination of mixed-gender and gender specific models. *Journal of Interpersonal Violence, 27*(12), 2322–2347.

Trammell, R. (2009). Values, rules, and keeping the peace: How men describe order and the inmate code in California prisons. *Deviant Behavior, 30*(8), 746–771.

Travis, J. (2011). Rethinking prison education in the era of mass incarceration. New York, NY: John Jay College of Criminal Justice, Keynote address.

Travis, L. F., & Edwards, B. D. (2015). *Introduction to criminal justice* (8th ed.). Waltham, MA: Anderson Publishing.

Treatment Advocacy Center. (2014). *The treatment of persons with mental illness in prisons and jails: A state survey.* Retrieved from: https://jpo.wrlc.org/bitstream/handle/11204/3553/The%20Treatment%20of%20Persons%20with%20Mental%20Illness%20in%20Prisons%20and%20Jails.pdf?sequence=4

Turner v. Safley, 482 US 78 (1987).

Umez, C., Cruz, J., Richey, M., & Albis, K. (2017). *Mentoring as a component of reentry: Practical considerations from the field.* New York, NY: The Council of State Governments Justice Center.

Varghese, F. P., Fitzgerald, E. L., Chronister, K. M., Cummings, D. L., & Forrest, L. (2013). Vocational psychology with criminal justice populations: Why not? *The Counseling Psychologist, 41*(7), 1072–1082.

Viglione, J., Rudes, D. S., & Taxman, F. S. (2017). Probation officer use of client-centered communication strategies in adult probation settings. *Journal of Offender Rehabilitation, 56,* 38–60.

Vox, F. (2016, December 9). We can no longer mask the barbarity of the death penalty. CNN. Retrieved from http://www.cnn.com/2016/12/09/opinions/we-can-no-longer-mask-barbarity-of-death-penalty-vox/index.html

Walsh v. Mellas, 837 F2d 789 (1988).

Wang, A., & Berman, M. (2018, April 17). Rioting leaves at least 7 dead, 17 hurt at S. Carolina prison. *Chicago Tribune,* p. 8.

Washington v. Harper, 494 US 210 (1990).

Whitehead, J. T., & Woodward, V. (2017). Ethical issues in probation, parole, and community corrections. In M. Braswell, B. McCarthy, & B. McCarthy (Eds.), *Justice, crime and ethics* (pp. 292–314). New York, NY: Routledge.

Whitehead, J. T., Dodson, K. D., & Edwards, B. D. (2013). *Corrections: Exploring crime, punishment, and justice in America.* Waltham, MA: Anderson.

Whitley v. Albers, 475 US 312 (1986).

Williams, B. A., Lindquist, K., Hill, T., Baillargeon, J., Mellow, J., Greifinger, R., & Walter, L. C. (2009). Caregiving behind bars: Correctional officer reports of disability in geriatric prisoners. *Journal of the American Geriatrics Society, 57,* 1286–1292.

Willison, J. B., Brazzell, D., & Kim, K. (2011). *Faith-based correctional and reentry programs: Advancing a conceptual framework for research and evaluation.* Washington, DC: The Urban Institute.

Wills, C. D. (2017). Right to counsel in juvenile court 50 years after In re Gault. *The Journal of the American Academy of Psychiatry and the Law, 45,* 140–144.

Wilson v. Seiter, 501 US 294 (1991).

Wodahl, E. J., & Garland, B. (2009). The evolution of community corrections: The enduring influence of the prison. *The Prison Journal, 89*(1), 81S–104S.

Wodahl, E. J., Boman, J. H., IV., & Garland, B. E. (2015). Responding to probation and parole violations: Are jail sanctions more effective than community-based graduated sanctions? *Journal of Criminal Justice, 43,* 242–250.

Wodahl, E. J., Ogle, R., Kadleck, C., & Gerow, K. (2013). Offender perceptions of graduated sanctions. *Crime & Delinquency, 59*(8), 1185–1210.

Wolff v. McDonnell, 418 US 539 (1974).

Wolff, N., Blitz, C. L., Shi, J., Siegel, J., & Bachman, R. (2007). Physical violence inside prisons: Rates of victimization. *Criminal Justice and Behavior, 34*(5), 588–599.

Wolff, N., Shi, J., & Siegel, J. A. (2009) Patterns of victimization among male and female inmates: Evidence of an enduring legacy. *Violence and Victims, 24*(4), 469–484.

Wooldredge, J., & Steiner, B. (2013). Violent victimization among state prison inmates. *Violence and Victims, 28*(3), 531–551.

Worley, R. M., & Worley, V. B. (2016). The economics of "crossing over": Examining the link between correctional officer pay and guard-inmate boundary violations. *Deviant Behavior, 37,* 16–29.

Worrall, J. L., & Morris, R. G. (2011). Inmate custody level and prison rule violations. *The Prison Journal, 91*(2), 131–157.

Yeh, S.S. (2010). Cost-benefit analysis of reducing crime through electronic monitoring of parolees and probationers. *Journal of Criminal Justice, 38,* 1090–1096.

Young, J. L., Antonio, M., & Wingeard, L. M. (2009). How staff attitude and support for inmate treatment and rehabilitation differs by job category: An evaluation of findings from Pennsylvania's department of corrections' employee training curriculum "reinforcing positive behavior." *Journal of Criminal Justice, 37,* 435–441.

Zapotsky, M. (2017, February 23). Justice department will again use private prisons. *The Washington Post.*

Zeng, Z. (2018). *Jail inmates in 2016.* Washington, DC: Bureau of Justice Statistics.

Zoukis, C. (2017). *Federal prison handbook: The definitive guide to surviving the federal bureau of prisons.* Sullivans Island, SC: Middle Street Publishing.